GW00393860

CC
£6
N Ane

The Mississippi Kite

NUMBER TWENTY-FIVE
THE CORRIE HERRING HOOKS SERIES

Richard L. Glinski

ERIC G. BOLEN
and
DAN FLORES

The
Mississippi Kite

Portrait of a Southern Hawk

UNIVERSITY OF TEXAS PRESS
AUSTIN

Requests for permission to reproduce material from this work should be sent to Permissions, University of Texas Press, Box 7819, Austin, TX 78713-7819.

∞ The paper used in this publication meets the minimum requirements of American National Standard for Information Sciences—Permanence of Paper for Printed Library Materials, ANSI Z39.48–1984.

Library of Congress Cataloging-in-Publication Data

Bolen, Eric G.
  The Mississippi kite / by Eric G. Bolen and Dan Flores. — 1st ed.
    p.   cm. — (The Corrie Herring Hooks series ; no. 25)
  Includes bibliographical references and index.
  ISBN 0-292-75148-6 (alk. paper)
    1. Mississippi kite. I. Flores, Dan L. (Dan Louie), date. II. Title.
III. Series.
QL696.F32B64 1993
598.9′16—dc20   93-3657

Frontispiece: Photo courtesy of Richard L. Glinski
Page vi: Photo courtesy of Wyman P. Meinzer
Page viii: Photo courtesy of Barbara Garland

Dedicated to the memory of

J. Knox Jones, Jr.
(1929–1992)

World-class biologist, faithful friend,
and staunch champion of research
as a pillar of academic vitality

Contents

Preface
ix

Acknowledgments
xi

The Mississippi Kite
1

Mississippi Kites in History
18

Breeding and Nesting
33

Raising Young
51

Food and Feeding
59

Conservation and Management
77

Appendix A. Common and Scientific Names of Plants and
Animals Mentioned in the Text
92

Appendix B. The Dimorphism Index
97

Appendix C. A Decade of Sightings by State
98

Readings and References
107

Preface

*W*hy a book about Mississippi Kites? There are at least three reasons.

First, they are lovely, sleek birds that, within their geographical distribution, often can be seen in either city or countryside. No need to don hipboots or cold-weather clothing, brave thorny brush or rocky slopes. Just look carefully from a convenient ranch road or a shady street of suburbia. In such places we can today find Mississippi Kites floating effortlessly in the sky just as explorer-naturalists saw them long ago.

Second, we have been fascinated with the history of events involving Mississippi Kites. And the colors of the historical palette are rich indeed. Like few other birds we know, the Mississippi Kite has been entwined with human history from the day of its scientific discovery early in the nineteenth century, through the government's make-work programs of the 1930s, to the urbanization of the American Southwest.

Finally, predators and predation remain riveting components of nature. Admittedly complex in its workings, many of which are still unclear to humans, predation has been a normal—and necessary—part of nature since the dawn of life. For us there is also the wondrous fascination with the give and take of the hungry and hunted, which surely represents one of the more thrilling segments of life outdoors. Too often the popular view of predation rests solely in images of blood-stained carcasses, overlooking the adaptations of predator and prey alike derived from eons of evolutionary testing in a dynamic laboratory. In the prejudiced mindset of many humans, we forget that predators include such "friendly" animals as robins and frogs, swallows and otters, as well as the more maligned species such as wolves and sharks. Or hawks.

All told, the Mississippi Kite is a wonderful bird with which to spend some time. Spare-time predators that we humans have been, the kite appeals to our instincts and evokes our ad-

[ix]

miration as a fulltime predator. Yet its chief prey is not moose or salmon or even rabbits, but insects. It has, at least at this end of its migratory route, an interesting, very classically North American story—one that is dynamic and still unfolding. It is an uncommonly lovely and graceful bird, yet sometimes is cursed by humans for being itself, a reaction as illogical as a rancher's dismay that coyotes ignore No Trespassing signs. Our editor, Shannon Davies, was told in Lubbock, Texas, in 1991 that Mississippi Kites were "trash birds," ostensibly because their ecological health on the High Plains is excellent and because they sometimes dive-bomb people. The more general reaction to Mississippi Kites is probably either ignorance or apathy. Neither does the kite justice.

Our format generally follows the biological calendar of Mississippi Kites, well laced with historical highlights. The book itself had its origins in friendship, in a mutually shared interest in nature, in a particular bird—and in an experiment. We wanted to see if a wildlife ecologist (a scientist) and an environmental historian (a humanist) could get along well enough to write a book together. And of course we hoped to produce a useful book in addition to continuing a long-standing friendship. In theory, a collaboration between authors apprenticed to such rather different views of the world ought to yield holistic insights rather than a singular view, but the veracity of that theory we happily leave to our readers. Aw, no matter. We had fun!

Acknowledgments

We want to acknowledge and thank those whose interest made this book possible: James P. McNab, for his expert translation of material originally written in French; the Olin Library at Cornell University, for providing McAtee's list of local names for kites; Danny Bystrak of the Bird Banding Laboratory of the U.S. Fish and Wildlife Service, for banding data; Terry Maxwell, for his counsel regarding kite research he supervised at Angelo State University in Texas; Glenn D. Swartz, for sharing with us his unpublished counts of kites migrating through southern Texas; J. Merrill Lynch, for his estimates of the kite population on the floodplain of the Roanoke River in North Carolina; John L. Trapp of the Office of Migratory Bird Management of the U.S. Fish and Wildlife Service, for details concerning the legislative history of hawk protection; Karen Steenhof of the Bureau of Land Management, for information about the Snake River Birds of Prey Area; Nancy J. Keeler, for materials about Hawk Mountain; the staffs of the William Madison Randall Library at the University of North Carolina at Wilmington and of the Texas Tech University Library in Lubbock, whose dedicated searches provided us with much-needed materials; Lisa I. Picklesimer, for locating citations in *American Birds*; Alda S. Ingram and Dan L. Noland, for their critical review of our text; Brian W. Cain, Richard C. Banks, Richard L. Glinski, Milton Friend, James F. Parnell, and Dan B. Boone, for sundry assistance; and Elizabeth D. Bolen, to whom one of us owes a measure of gratitude that words alone cannot express.

ERIC G. BOLEN
WILMINGTON, NORTH CAROLINA

DAN L. FLORES
YELLOW HOUSE CANYON, TEXAS

[xi]

When viewed overhead, the appearance of a Mississippi Kite is not unlike the familiar comic book logo of Batman suspended in the sky. Kites of all species are aptly named for their buoyant flight. Photo courtesy of Dan Flores.

The Mississippi Kite

First Contact

*P*eter Custis, just 25 years old and on leave from medical school in Philadelphia, waded ashore. Behind him, several oarsmen rested in a flat-bottomed boat temporarily beached on a convenient sandbar in the shallow channel. Moments before, Custis had spotted an unusual bird and quickly halted the expedition from its tedious advance up the Red River. The location was somewhere above the old French city of Natchitoches, Louisiana, perhaps just north of where maps today locate Shreveport. The year was 1806, and enduring fame was about to befall Meriwether Lewis and William Clark for their heroic 8,000-mile journey across the unknown tracts of western America. Now, in the summer of the same year, another government-sponsored excursion was under way into Mr. Jefferson's newly acquired *terra incognita*.

Custis reached shore and entered the towering cottonwood forest bordering the river. Seconds later a blast from his shotgun felled the sleek-bodied bird, which was soon prepared as yet one more specimen of the "natural productions" of the vast Louisiana Territory. A few days later, on 1 July 1806, during a respite at a Creek Indian village, Custis scribbled in his report only brief mention of the bird, "A species of *Falco* which I have not seen described." For technical reasons peculiar to the arcane science of taxonomy, credit for his discovery would go elsewhere, and Custis himself soon would fade into obscurity. Yet President Jefferson's young naturalist had collected not a falcon but a Mississippi Kite, and in the process had introduced a remarkable bird to Western science.

2

Appearance in the Field

Nearly two centuries later and some 500 miles west of the site where Peter Custis first saw and described the Mississippi Kite, we stand on the rimrock of a wide, shallow canyon scored into the flat surface of the Southern High Plains. Tall cottonwoods shimmer and black willows roll in the morning breeze. The line of trees marks the course of a spring-fed tributary trickling down the canyon floor to a larger stream. The gallery forest is nearly half a mile below us, but in the transparent air of the plains we can clearly see a half-dozen falconlike birds floating leisurely over the trees, slowly tracing out trackless paths of odd, octagonlike circles. One bird soars higher than the others. Seen from below, for the moment stalled in a gust of wind, its silhouette looks for all the world like the Batman logo suspended in the sky. There's no mystery that kites were named for their buoyant and airy flight. We quickly focus our binoculars for a closer look.

Several field marks identify a Mississippi Kite: its pointed wings, clearly angled and nearly 3 feet tip to tip; a long, dark tail rectangular in outline (neither wedge shaped nor pointed) with just a hint of a notch at its tip; a gray underside; and a light, almost white head with a pronounced black mask across its eyes. In good light, we might glimpse a tint of chestnut on some of the larger wing feathers and, up close, a relatively delicate black bill. The piercing stare of scarlet eyes glaring from the dark mask gives the Mississippi Kite its distinctive countenance. We are watching an adult, but under field conditions it is seldom possible to distinguish males from females by size, coloration, or behavior.

Later in the summer, as the heat builds and the plains yellow, nesting will end, and we will encounter juveniles as well as adults. The body plumage of the young birds is streaked and appears more brown than gray, but the wings are dark, as in the adults. Juveniles lack the striking white head plumage they will acquire later. For now, their heads are dusky and streaked. Seen from below, circling on set wings, the juveniles can be identified by their tails, which are crossed with distinctive white bars—the best field mark. Close up, we would find that a young kite's eyes are brown and that the cere—the fleshy bump at the base of the bill—is bright yellow, which will gradually turn to jet black with maturity.

3
Voice

Mississippi Kites utter a piercing "phee phew" whistle, with the accent on the clipped first syllable. The second syllable is extended and slurs downward. The call is the same in both sexes.

A second call, more intimate, has been described as chippering. It consists of the "phee" followed by three or more softer repetitions of the same syllable. Sherri Evans, who studied Mississippi Kites in southern Illinois, reports five contexts where chippering is used: (*a*) by females when soliciting food from their mates as part of the behavior associated with pair-bond maintenance, (*b*) by females after copulation, (*c*) during nest construction, by both sexes, (*d*) at nest relief, when the birds replace one another during incubation, and (*e*) between adults and their nestlings.

4
Other Names

W. L. McAtee, renowned federal biologist from 1904 to 1947 and first editor (in 1937) of the *Journal of Wildlife Management*, compiled over his lifetime (1883–1962) a monumental list of common names for American birds. These records remain the foremost source of its kind and were consulted for the following list:

In various books, Mississippi Kites have been called

American kite	blue snake-hawk	blue kite
hawk of the South	hovering kite	lead kite
Louisiana kite	Louisiana blue kite	square-tailed
Mississippi ictinia	spotted-tailed hobby	kite

Folk names in various parts of the species' range include

blue darter (Miss., La., Okla., Tex.)   blue hawk (Okla.)
grasshopper hawk (Ga., Tex.)   locust-eater (La.)
locust hawk (Okla.)   mosquito hawk
pigeon hawk (Ga.)   (Ala., Miss.)
snake-killer hawk (Tex.)   rabbit hawk (Fla.)

McAtee's list of names, while indeed rich and colorful, represents some fact and a good deal of fancy. Mississippi Kites indeed do capture large numbers of locusts and grasshoppers, but it is highly doubtful that the birds hunt for prey as large as rabbits and pigeons (i.e., "locust hawk" is apt, whereas "rabbit hawk" is not). Perhaps snakes, if not too large, are a small part of their diet, but while it certainly would be a dramatic event to witness, snake catching is probably so rare that "snake-killer hawk" or "blue snake-hawk" are largely ill-founded misnomers. On the other hand, "hovering kite" reflects a commonplace hunting posture of Mississippi Kites, a trait shared with a delightful relative, the American Kestrel—itself a species once known with considerable inaccuracy as the "sparrow hawk."

"Hawk of the South" originated from no less a figure than the famed painter John James Audubon, who encountered the species during his southern travels, but we must note that all species of kites occurring in the United States are southern birds (see following). Indeed, "American kite" better reflects the much wider distribution of the Mississippi Kite in the United States not only throughout the South, but in the Southwest, Midwest, and mid-Atlantic states as well.

The descriptive name "square-tailed kite" is fairly applied to Mississippi Kites, although the tail of another American species—the Black-shouldered Kite—is no different in shape, albeit much unlike in color. By comparison, the tails of the two remaining American kites are quite dissimilar in shape. "Spotted-tailed hobby" seems quite out of place, unless one accepts the unlikely observation that the bars on the tail of a Mississippi Kite in juvenile plumage somehow represent spots.

We close this section by noting what by now may be obvious; namely, that common names of birds (and other organisms) are often confusing and even inaccurate. McAtee's list, for example, includes "pigeon hawk" for Mississippi Kites (at least in Georgia), but this is also the widely used common name for a species of falcon that professional ornithologists formally call the Merlin—and which, by any name, seldom preys on pigeons! Another falcon does feed regularly on pigeons, but, true to form, the Peregrine Falcon is often known as a "duck hawk." Because of such confusion, scientists issue Latin names for each species of organism and for the respective groups to which each species belongs. Moreover, as noted above, the identification of a particular state might imply that Mississippi Kites are limited in distribution, as indeed is true of Everglade Kites in the United States. But the selection of "Mississippi" in the kite's name simply reflects the locale where the first specimen was collected and given its scientific name. Even so, as we shall see later, "Mississippi" as a descriptor for this species of kite is no more than a quirk of history. Had fate worked otherwise, we instead might know the species today by a name such as Louisiana or Red River kite.

5
Distribution

The breeding range of Mississippi Kites includes the southeastern and Gulf states, as well as large areas in the interior. The species is migratory and, at the completion of the breeding season, flocks of Mississippi Kites leave the United States for a winter stay in South America.

Some words about bird banding may be useful here. John James Audubon is credited as the first to band birds in North America when he attached "silver thread" to the legs of birds. Today, tens of thousands of birds are banded each year by scores of amateur and professional ornithologists using individually numbered aluminum bands, and large computers manage the immense volume of data resulting from those efforts.

Of the information gleaned from banding operations, the most obvious concerns the distribution and movements of birds. Unfortunately, those bands that are recovered represent only a small percentage of the number of birds actually banded. Most banded birds die in obscurity, quite without the generosity of lending any information to science. Even when a relatively large number of people may be in contact with certain groups of birds—as with duck hunters, for example—the recovery rate seldom exceeds 10 percent. The recovery rate for other birds is usually nearer 1 percent. For the latter, including Mississippi Kites, 1,000 birds would have to be captured and banded to yield just 10 band recoveries, which is clearly a meager sample on which to base biological conclusions. The latter ratio is, in fact, just about the actual case. Records maintained at the Bird Banding Laboratory operated by the U.S. Fish and Wildlife Service indicate that of 855 Mississippi Kites banded by the end of 1991, exactly 10 (1.17 percent) have been recovered.

Most Mississippi Kites are banded as nestlings. The young kites, of course, must be large enough before a leg band of the appropriate size can be attached, thereby assuring a lifetime means of identification. Contrary to popular opinion, handling young kites (or other birds) does not cause rejection by their parents. The sense of smell in birds is too poor for human odors to jeopardize the bond between parent and offspring as sometimes may happen with mammals.

Adult kites are harder to capture for banding, although Denice Shaw has developed an exciting technique that often works satisfactorily, especially near nesting sites. She took advantage of the kites' dislike for Great Horned Owls and tethered a living owl on loan from a rehabilitation center for wounded birds in front of a "mist net," a device for capturing birds that resembles a huge hair net stretched between two poles. Disturbed by the presence of a feared predator, the attacking kites become harmlessly but decidedly entangled when they attack the owl. Kites thus entrapped are removed from the net, banded, and immediately released. Our own field tests in Texas using a molded plastic owl decoy left both us and the kites convinced that a counterfeit owl is no substitute for the real thing. We emphasize that it is illegal to capture kites and other wild birds for any purpose, including banding, without appropriate state and federal permits.

Despite the instructions imprinted on each band—"Avise Bird Band Write Washington, D.C. USA"—the chances of learning about a banded bird decrease considerably when it is recovered in another country. Illiteracy, the cost of postage, and perhaps the simple pleasure of retaining the band as a keepsake often limit the flow of data.

In any case, precious few banded kites have been recovered outside the United States from which we might learn more about the wintering grounds of Mississippi Kites. Sight records made on living birds in the field may be inconclusive because a look-alike species, the Plumbeous Kite, also occurs in Latin America. Only the cocksure ornithologist of the last century, John Cassin, thought the birds were, in his words, "quite different" in appearance, adding that "a comparison of specimens of the two species would render a suspicion of their [similarity] quite impossible." Cassin's opinion has gained virtually no currency in the intervening years, however, and the current edition of the *Check-list of North American Birds*, published by the American Ornithologists' Union, in fact suggests the birds might be regarded as a single species in the future. Nonetheless, an adult Mississippi Kite banded in a residential area in San Angelo, Texas, was recovered on a November day two years later in a semihumid lowland forest in eastern Bolivia. Another individual, banded as a nestling in Oklahoma, was recovered the following October in Guatemala and apparently represents the recovery of a bird still in transit southward. The only other record from Latin America concerns a kite recovered in Honduras in March, eight months after it was banded in Kansas, when it was probably en route back to the United States.

The banding data are supplemented by a few museum specimens of birds collected in Latin America. These permit the requisite in-hand inspection for the subtle differences in plumage that separate Mississippi and Plumbeous kites. E. R. Blake of the Chicago Natural History Museum conducted such a search for kite specimens and uncovered two winter records (December and February) from Paraguay. The collector of the two birds reported that Mississippi Kites usually arrive in Paraguay between October and February, most often after a period of stormy weather. Later, an ornithologist at the American Museum of Natural History discovered a specimen collected in Argentina in January.

Much more remains to be learned about the movements and wintertime destinations of Mississippi Kites. Quite remarkably, the discovery in 1949 of specimens collected in Paraguay extended the known limits of the winter range of Mississippi Kites by 4000 miles! For now, the banding and specimen records at hand indicate that, instead of migrating across the Gulf of Mexico, the birds travel the length of the Central American isthmus and winter well into the interior of southern South America. These records dispel the older belief that, except for stragglers, the birds regularly overwinter in Florida, Texas, and Central America.

Whereas much about the winter quarters of Mississippi Kites remains unknown or uncertain, we can describe with more confidence the extent of their breeding range in the United States. Even so, Mississippi Kites are among those organisms with a generous degree of plasticity—the ability to adapt to various environmental settings—and thus represent a species whose breeding range remains dynamic.

The southeastern range of Mississippi Kites suggests a broad arc extending from Texas eastward along the Gulf Coast, across Georgia, and ending almost precisely on the border between South Carolina and North Carolina. Most of peninsular Florida is excluded, parts of which are the exclusive domain of Everglade Kites. Northward, kites range into the farmlands and pastures of Kansas and Oklahoma, not excluding those winding stretches of riparian woodlands still intact in the heartland

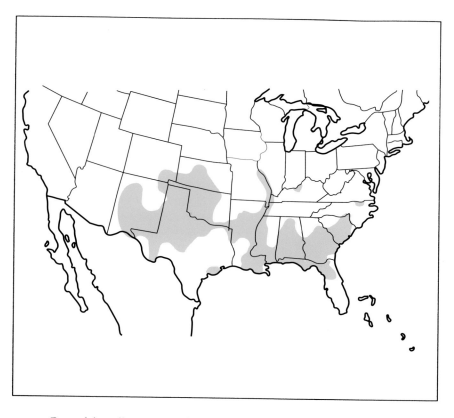

General breeding range of Mississippi Kites in the United States. Sightings also regularly occur in many other states, including northern North Carolina and the Cape May area of New Jersey, but nesting in these areas has not been confirmed (see Appendix C). Map adapted from various sources compiled by Ralph S. Palmer.

of the Great Plains. The map also reveals a spur projecting upward from the arc, extending the breeding range well up into the Mississippi Valley to southern Illinois. The tip of this projection represents an area where the breeding range of Mississippi Kites seems fluid but gradually expanding.

Perhaps the most dynamic area in the breeding range of Mississippi Kites occurs in the southwestern United States. Whereas kites have appeared regularly for several decades in the western half of Texas, the birds in recent years have nested in New Mexico and in selected areas of Arizona. A nesting record for Arizona, apparently the first, was reported in 1970 along the San Pedro River. Altogether, as many as 10 pairs of kites may have nested that year in the riparian woodlands bordering the San Pedro's course to the Gila River. Other records from 1970 and 1973, including a specimen with a fully developed egg, confirmed the presence of breeding kites in Arizona. One authority, familiar with the Gila and its tributaries, suggests that the enormous populations of cicadas in the saltcedar understory of the riparian woodlands may account for the kite's distribution in Arizona.

An isolated population representing what biologists call a disjunct distribution occurs in the vicinity of Scotland Neck along the Roanoke River in northern North Carolina. The birds thus skip over almost the entire north-south axis of North Carolina to settle in Roanoke's floodplain. Field biologists familiar with the region have counted at least 30 Mississippi Kites at one time, which they suspect may be only one-third of the total population in residence along the Roanoke River. The late-summer population at Scotland Neck regularly includes kites in juvenile plumage but, to date, no one has discovered a nest.

Numerous other records of Mississippi Kites dot the geography of the United States, enough to indicate a more-or-less wandering coterie of individuals or perhaps an annual probe into as yet uncolonized regions. Among these we mention sightings of kites along the northeastern seaboard in New Jersey where, although the observations are of growing regu-

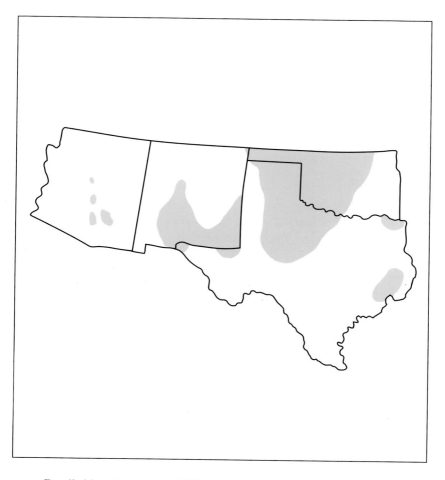

Detailed breeding range of Mississippi Kites in the American Southwest, where their expanding distribution has been particularly dynamic in New Mexico and Arizona since the 1950s. Map adapted from the work of Richard L. Glinski and Antonio L. Gennaro.

larity, they are so far unaccompanied by confirmed records of nesting activities. One authority on the birds of Cape May suggests that these occurrences result when long-distance migrants "overshoot" their traditional breeding grounds. Whatever the cause, it may well be just a matter of time before kites begin serious housekeeping in these extralimital areas—the biological term for sites outside the usual distribution of a species— thereby extending the species' breeding range northward by several hundred miles.

6
Other Kites in the United States

Along with kites, scientists include all of the world's hawks, eagles, and falcons in Accipitridae, a family in the order Falconiformes. Within Accipitridae are more than 200 species, but our interest centers on the Mississippi Kite, known formally to science as *Ictinia mississippiensis* and, in passing, on three other kites that regularly occur across the United States. Many other species of kites occur throughout the world, but these must be ignored here.

The Everglade Kite, also known as the Snail Kite, is widespread in much of Mexico and Central and South America (see Appendix A for the scientific names of this and other species mentioned in the text). In the United States, however, the species is restricted to the Everglades Basin and a few other freshwater areas in Florida. The birds are nonmigratory and remain in Florida year-round. The Everglade Kite is on the federal endangered species list because so few occur in the United States. Unlike that of the other species of kites occurring in the United States, the flight pattern of Everglade Kites is "floppy" rather than graceful, and their food habits are highly specialized. Their diet, as suggested by their alternate name, is limited to snails. In fact, Everglade Kites specialize on a single species, the apple snail, from which the birds extract the soft parts with long, sharply hooked bills.

Everglade Kites are dark and have broad wings. Their tails are wedge-shaped and on males are white with a broad black band near the trailing edge. Females are brown and streaked, and their tails are not as clearly marked as those of the males.

Another kite occurring in the United States is the Black-shouldered Kite. This kite frequents open country in three widely separated parts of the United States: the southern tip of Florida, southern Texas, and the low coastal areas of Oregon and California. The species is not migratory, but sightings outside of these areas, in such widely separated places as New Mexico and South Carolina, are not unusual. Various forms of the species occur over a vast area of the globe, including Central and South America, southern Europe, Arabia, Africa, southeastern Asia, Australia, and groups of islands such as the Philippines and East Indies.

These birds have well-defined black shoulder patches, as their name implies, on light gray wings. Their backs are gray, but the remainder of the body plumage of adults is white. The tail is white and, like that of the Mississippi Kite, is long and rectangular with a faint suggestion of a notched tip (until recently, the species was known as the white-tailed kite). The sexes are alike in appearance.

The American Swallow-tailed Kite prefers low, often swampy areas in the coastal plains of the southeastern and Gulf states from South Carolina to Texas. Swallow-tailed Kites are migratory and, after breeding, move through Mexico and the Greater Antilles to winter quarters in Colombia, Venezuela, and other areas of South America.

This species is perhaps the most stunning in appearance among the kites occurring in the United States. Its plumage displays a striking contrast of black and white: white head; black back; white underside; and wings black above, but white underneath with black tips and edges. The most notable feature, however, is the deeply forked tail (also black) whose tips are spread widely in flight. Each pointed apex of the fork extends well beyond the folded wing tips when the bird is perched. Males and females are alike in plumage.

[13]

The Hook-billed Kite, a nonmigratory species normally occurring in Mexico, Cuba, and Central and South America, has at times appeared and nested just inside the borders of the United States. A nest was discovered on the Santa Ana National Wildlife Refuge in Texas, within a few yards of the Rio Grande's northern bank.

We introduce here the term *raptor*, which refers to birds of prey and includes all of the hawks, eagles, falcons, kites, and related forms—as well as all species of owls. Vultures, although scavengers, are also considered raptors because of their taxonomic affinities with the group that includes the hawks. Hence, two rather dissimilar orders of birds—hawks and their allies in Falconiformes and owls in Strigiformes—are collectively known as raptors. Whether shrikes, also birds of prey and representing yet another group of birds, might also be covered by the umbrella of the term remains arguable. *Raptor* itself is etymologically derived from *raptus*, a form of the Latin verb *rapere*, meaning "to seize." We hope it is clear, therefore, that *raptor* has an ecological basis as a term describing feeding behavior and has nothing to do with avian taxonomy.

7
Relationship of Kites with Other Hawks

Subgroups within the avian order Falconiformes are difficult to organize to the satisfaction of all taxonomists. However, one system recognizes three major suborders: one that combines the vultures of the New World (Catharatae), another that unites the falcons and caracaras (Falcones), and a third group (Accipitres) that includes three families:

Sagittariidae—Secretary Bird (1 species)
Pandionidae—Osprey (1 species)
Accipitridae—a large group consisting of the kites, hawks, eagles, and Old World vultures (about 270 species, depending on the taxonomic authority consulted)

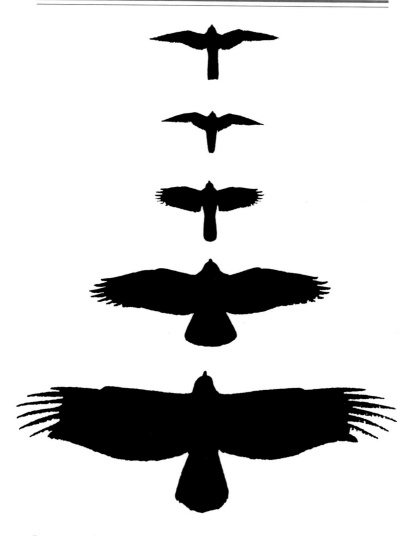

Representative silhouettes of selected types of raptors. From top to bottom are kites, falcons, accipiters, buteos, and eagles. Kites and falcons both have pointed wings and long tails, but falcons are powerful fliers, whereas kites glide bouyantly. Sizes for some species within each type may be larger or smaller than species in other groups, but the shapes shown here hold true for all species within each type. Check field guides for identifications of individual species, including ospreys, owls, and other kinds of raptors.

Most of the groups within Accipitridae have distinctive outlines. Accipiters such as the Cooper's Hawk have short rounded wings and long tails. Hawks include familiar roadside species such as the Red-tailed Hawk, which is typical of the buteos—those hawks with thickset bodies, wide tails, and broad wings. Eagles are little more than very large buteos. The streamlined falcons, in suborder Falcones, have relatively long tails and sharply pointed wings. A glance at any of the popular field guides will reveal these differences to even a casual observer of birds.

Within Accipitridae, kites may be the most primitive members of the family. That is, kites may most closely resemble the ancestral stock from which hawks and others in the family later evolved.

Kites themselves are subdivided into three subunits based on their anatomical differences:

Those with a bony shield projecting above the eyes, which contributes to their fierce-looking appearance. Their talons are ungrooved and flat or somewhat rounded on the underside. This group includes the Black-shouldered Kite.

A diverse group also with an eye shield, but all having the basal joint of the middle toe fused with the next joint. This group includes the Everglade Kite and the Mississippi Kite.

Those lacking an eye shield, a group that includes the Swallow-tailed Kite.

While science continues to grapple with the taxonomy, distribution, and habits of kites, for most observers of the Mississippi Kite the quintessential reality is simply that the bird *exists.* Wherever it is found, the Mississippi Kite is a beautiful and fascinating member of the natural world. In what follows, we have tried to capture both the aesthetic qualities and the life history of this intriguing bird of prey—our portrait of a southern hawk.

Immature Mississippi Kite. The description (see text) recorded in the 1806 journal of Peter Custus matches the bird shown here except for the still-yellow ceres, which will become black as the bird reaches full maturity. Photo courtesy of Wyman P. Meinzer.

Mississippi Kites in History

I
Western Exploration and Discovery of the Mississippi Kite

*T*hrough a fortuitous accident of ecology and history, the Mississippi Kite was one of those species—along with the prairie dogs, pronghorn, coyote, grizzly bear, and magpies—that lay directly in the path of the nineteenth-century exploration of the American West. Beginning in 1803 and extending into the 1870s and 1880s, first the War Department and then the U.S. Geological Survey sent almost 100 expeditions into the alien, arid interior of the continent. Naturalists accompanying these explorations conducted their searches along the rivers and into the badlands and canyons of the Great Plains, across the highest passes of the Rockies and the Sierra Nevada, and into the deserts and slickrock gorges of the Southwest.

In their traditional summer breeding range, Mississippi Kites hunted and nested not only in the rimswamps bordering the lower Mississippi but also along the eastern perimeter of the Southern Great Plains. Their distribution and strong ecological association with riparian habitats meant that kites were likely to be encountered early on by explorer-naturalists following major rivers across the prairies. Kite colonies evidently were a widely scattered but highly visible local component of the original wilderness ecosystems formed by rivers such as the Red and its tributaries, the two forks of the Canadian, and the Arkansas. Given this setting, it is scarcely startling that the very first major expedition to ascend one of these rivers can be credited with introducing the Mississippi Kite to science—and to subsequent environmental history.

Thomas Jefferson had longed to unlock the unimagined secrets of the American interior since at least the early 1790s, when he had several times attempted to sponsor private expeditions westward. Upon acquiring the Louisiana Territory from a French government disillusioned with New World ventures,

American Ornithology (1811), he omitted any mention of either Custis or Bartram.

One additional touch of irony in the relationship between Wilson and Custis probably had occurred in February 1809 when the painter visited New Bern, North Carolina, on his southern tour. While there, Wilson sold subscriptions for *American Ornithology* to two of that town's leading citizens, John Devereaux and William Gaston. Given that Wilson surely sought the patronage of the more wealthy residents, which Devereaux and Gaston certainly were, for his relatively expensive volumes, there seems little doubt that Dr. Custis, late of the Red River Expedition and now a physician in New Bern, would have been on Wilson's list of prospective subscribers. Wilson had yet to reach Dunbar's plantation for his fateful encounter with a Mississippi Kite, but he may well have had some interesting dialogue with Custis about other birds of the western territories. We shall never know, of course, what, if any, conversation occurred in New Bern between the two men. What is sure, however, is that, unlike two of his neighbors, Peter Custis did not subscribe to Wilson's future volume with its striking plate of a Mississippi Kite.

The first Mississippi Kite Wilson shot became immortalized not only because of its dramatic portrait—often considered one of the best paintings in *American Ornithology*—but also because of Wilson's account of the experience. Reaching to retrieve the wounded bird, Wilson found the palm of his hand impaled by one of the bird's razor-sharp talons, so that he was unable to paint for several days. While he nursed both himself and the crippled kite, he observed the bird's habits closely, an experience that produced a memorable passage in *American Ornithology*: "The whole time he lived with me, he seemed to watch every movement I made; erecting the feathers of his hind head, and eyeing me with savage fierceness; considering me, no doubt, as the greater savage of the two." Wilson went on to shoot at least three other kites for examination (he never collected a female), although which of the four became the type specimen is now unknown. In the English ornithological journal *Ibis*, John Cassin in 1860 referred to "Wilson's original" as one of six kite skins then on deposit at the Academy of Natural Sciences in Philadelphia.

The decade and a half following Jefferson's aborted Red River exploration into the Southwest saw three expeditions traverse the heart of the Mississippi Kite's summer range. One, the party dispatched by American General James Wilkinson and commanded by Lieutenant Zebulon Montgomery Pike, traveled west along the Arkansas River—the northwestern perimeter of the kite's range—in the year 1807. Along with several hazy political objectives that are still not clear but suggest an American-inspired coup aimed at the northern Spanish provinces, Pike was directed to observe the natural history of the Louisiana Territory. As might befit a spy, however, "neither my education nor my taste led me to the pursuit," as Pike phrased it, and no biological data accordingly resulted from his southwestern venture. A second, private exploration by Thomas Nuttall led this now-famous botanist onto the waters of the lower Arkansas in present-day Arkansas and Oklahoma in the summer of 1819. Although Nuttall traversed what was presumably excellent Mississippi Kite habitat and did it at the right time of year, he includes no notice of kites from a large swath of country between the Arkansas and the middle Red. Such negative evidence may indicate that kite populations in the original wilderness were localized, or perhaps fluctuated from year to year, possibly in response to prey availability.

This conclusion seems further strengthened by the experiences of the third southwestern exploration of this period, that of Stephen Long and Edwin James. The Long Expedition crossed the plains to the Central Rockies in 1820. After a cursory examination of the Front Range, Long divided his party, sending one contingent, led by Captain John Bell and including naturalist Thomas Say, down the Arkansas, while he, along with illustrator Titian Peale and James, the botanist and chronicler of the exploration, took a small party in search of the headwaters of the Red River. Instead, they struck the Canadian. During August and September they traversed most of the Canadian's drainage from eastern New Mexico through present Oklahoma, but only once did they report kites. On 15 August 1820, just northwest of the present town of Canadian in the Texas Panhandle, Long's men twice crossed the river. On that day, as James described it,

> Several species of locust were extremely frequent here, filling the air by day with their shrill and deafening cries, and feeding with their bodies great numbers of that beautiful species of hawk, the Falco *Mississippiensis* of Wilson. It afforded us a constant amusement to watch the motions of this greedy devourer, in the pursuit of the locust his favorite prey. The insect being large and not very active is easily taken; the hawk then poises on the wing, suspending himself in the air, while with his talons and beak he tears in pieces and devours his prey.

Again, here was an expedition that followed prime kite habitat—the riparian woodlands along the rivers of the southern prairies—and did indeed see "great numbers" of Mississippi Kites. Still, Long and his colleagues found kites only in one spot, during what would seem to have been a cicada bloom. Noteworthy, too, was the fact that Long did not see kites until east of the Llano Estacado, after the party had entered the range of persimmon trees, black walnuts, bobwhites, and blue jays. Regrettably, Peale's journal for this part of the exploration has been lost, as was Thomas Say's journal, when some members of the party deserted while descending the Arkansas. Captain Bell had no interest in natural history, and his journal contains no mention of kites or any other birds along the Arkansas River.

During the summer following the return of the Long Expedition, the Mississippi Kite colonies in Louisiana were visited by still another American naturalist. In 1821, John James Audubon had not yet emerged as Alexander Wilson's great rival in American bird study. Nonetheless, Audubon already was collecting specimens and preparing original drawings for *The Birds of America*, still more than a decade away from publica-

Plates of Mississippi Kites by Alexander Wilson (left) and John James Audubon (right). Wilson's painting is based on a male he wounded near Natchez, Mississippi, and appeared in his multivolume *American Ornithology* more than a decade before Audubon's sketches were made for *The Birds of America*. Audubon's "female" (lower bird) is plagiarized—as a mirror image!—from Wilson's plate. Three warblers adorn the edges of Wilson's plate. Photos courtesy of the Library of Congress.

tion. In June of 1821, as Audubon journeyed from New Orleans to Bayou Sara, he wrote with some frustration in his journal: "The long-wished for Mississippi kite and Swallow-tailed kite hovered over us. But our guns were packed . . ." He had first seen Mississippi Kites, according to his account, in 1819, but his stay at the Pirrie Plantation on Bayou Sara finally provided an opportunity to add a specimen to his collection. On 28 June 1821, a blast from Audubon's shotgun at last fetched a kite out of the humid, leadened skies of West Feliciana Parish. At hand was a beautiful, mature male, which Audubon proceeded to render from life using his own blend of pencil, pastels, and watercolor.

The plate of Audubon's Mississippi Kite was not published until 1831, and the controversy over it further fueled the Wilson-Audubon rivalry. The plate featured two kites, supposedly a pair (both birds were actually males). The problem arose from an obvious plagiarism. The lower "female" bird in Audubon's plate was an exact copy, albeit reversed, of the male kite in Wilson's *American Ornithology!* Wilson had died in 1813, but his biographer, George Ord, lost no time bringing the matter to the attention of anyone who would listen. Nonetheless, in his role as the American Noble Savage incarnate, John James Audubon was too attractive a figure to be much tarnished by the charge. And as some of his biographers have pointed out, Audubon in any case probably was not entirely responsible. He seems to have submitted to his engraver only the upper bird, which he had drawn in Louisiana in 1821. Still, Audubon must carry a good measure of blame for this episode: obviously he did not censor the work when his engraver finished the composition with a "female" lifted directly from Wilson's earlier work.

During the 1840s, the Army Corps of Topographical Engineers sponsored a new wave of western expeditions, of which several were commanded by the dashing and complicated egomaniac John Charles Fremont. Charged on one of his later expeditions to examine the Southern High Plains, Fremont instead sent Lieutenant James W. Abert from Bent's Fort to the upper Canadian, which the intrepid young lieutenant followed eastward to its confluence with the Arkansas River in 1845.

Abert, who evidently enjoyed birds, thus traveled directly into the heart of Mississippi Kite country. Nonetheless, Abert did not report seeing any Mississippi Kites, probably because the expeditions did not enter the Texas Panhandle until September, apparently just after all the kites at that latitude had migrated south.

3
The Pacific Railroad Surveys and After

If the negative evidence from Abert's journey confirms modern observations about the timing of kite migrations, Samuel W. Woodhouse, surgeon and naturalist to the two Sitgreaves expeditions, presents an additional argument that colonies of Mississippi Kites appeared in patches across the species' summer range. This, at least, was Woodhouse's experience when he traversed the Indian Territory with the Sitgreaves survey of the Creek Boundary in 1849. Near the falls of the Verdigris River he found "the Mississippi kite (*Ictinia plumbea*) very abundant[.] Its food consisted principally of locusts[.]" Woodhouse reported no other observations of kites, although he returned with the survey party under Lieutenant I. C. Woodruff the following year. He seems to have collected and preserved at least three Mississippi Kites from these two expeditions, although their skins would later erroneously be listed in the Academy of Natural Sciences of Philadelphia as part of a "New Mexico" fauna. The confusion stemmed from Woodhouse's assignment to the Sitgreaves Expedition on the Zuni and Colorado rivers in 1851–1852 and subsequent publication of his natural history work from all three expeditions in the official report of the last. Woodhouse was certainly familiar with Mississippi Kites by the time he accompanied Sitgreaves into present-day Arizona, but he reported no kites in his 1851–1852 journals, although today kites are highly visible in that same country.

But on the Canadian River of New Mexico, Texas, and Oklahoma, where Stephen Long had reported colonies of kites in

1820, at least one other mid-century naturalist did see kites. And his description presents something of a puzzle, one of those firsthand observations from the wilderness that doesn't fit the pattern of other evidence.

The 35th Parallel Road Survey of 1853 along the Canadian River was led by Lieutenant Amiel Whipple, a capable explorer who unfortunately couldn't correctly add his own figures—else his route would have been selected for the Transcontinental Railroad! Whipple's troop included Heinrich Baldwin Moll-hausen, a protégé of the world-renowned explorer-author Alexander von Humboldt. Like several other nineteenth-century Europeans, Mollhausen would use his experiences in the West to become a Romantic novelist of American wilderness life. Indeed, Mollhausen's career served as an inspiration for famous Karl May, Germany's "Zane Grey." Mollhausen's Romantic conception of the Prairie Sublime was already fully in place by 1853. His *Diary of a Journey*, replete with stunning—and often fanciful—illustrations from his own hand, became a minor nature classic.

That Mollhausen saw Mississippi Kites along the Canadian there can be no doubt. The problem is with the timing and location of his description. The sixteenth of September 1853, along the river somewhere northwest of present Amarillo, was a spectacular day that had begun with a prairie aurora, a sunrise preceded by a crown of rays fingering the dawn sky. How much of what Mollhausen wrote about that day was romance and how much was reality is hard to say, but his description included this scene:

> Antelope were springing about on the dry hills, deer lurking behind the blue-green cedars, eagles and kites wheeling their flight through the air, and lively little prairie dogs peeping out and giving tongue from the openings of their dark abodes.

Not only is mid-September quite late to see kites at this latitude in the Texas Panhandle, but this also—if accepted as fact—represents the most westerly sighting of Mississippi Kites during the exploration era. We suspect that Mollhausen may have embellished his scenario on this date with the addition of birds he in fact had seen both earlier and farther downriver. And yet, even if his description is a case of generic prose painting, it definitely includes the Mississippi Kite as one of the fixed icons of the prairie wilderness.

Strikingly, of all the naturalists who accompanied expeditions traversing Texas, the Indian Territory, and the Southwest during the period of the Mexican Boundary and 1850s Pacific Railroad surveys, only Samuel Woodhouse collected Mississippi Kites. In 1858, Spencer Baird summarized the reports of 15 exploring parties and a host of other collectors from the West in his volume *Birds*, drawn up for the *Reports of the Explorations and Surveys*. At least four naturalists, including Dr. T. C. Henry of the 32nd Parallel Survey, made significant bird collections in the Mississippi Kite's range. Nonetheless, Woodhouse's specimens from present-day Oklahoma were the only Mississippi Kites collected! And, as Baird noted, Woodhouse had confused the kites he saw with their tropical relatives, Plumbeous Kites.

In our opinion, the most intriguing evidence that the summer distribution of Mississippi Kites changed dramatically during the last century originates from a little-known expedition that combed the canyonland wilderness at the headwaters of the Red River in 1876. In that year, Lieutenant Ernest Ruffner executed a thorough reconnaissance of the Red River's origins, the region Marcy supposedly had explored in 1852. A hidden wonderland sawed by flowing water into more than a dozen major canyons, with 60-mile-long Palo Duro Canyon at its heart, this diverse ecosystem today harbors numerous large colonies of Mississippi Kites. Indeed, a modern hiker packing through remote sections of Palo Duro Canyon can easily see two or three dozen kites at a time circling the cottonwood gallery along the Prairie Dog Town Fork of the Red River. Charles McCauley, the careful and diligent ornithologist attached to the Ruffner Expedition, spent more than a month in 1876 searching these canyons where he saw a variety of raptors: Bald Eagles, Ospreys, Swainson's Hawks, Red-tailed Hawks,

American Kestrels, Merlins, Prairie Falcons, even a Swallow-tailed Kite. Yet McCauley does not report seeing a single Mississippi Kite in Palo Duro Canyon, a telling omission since his surveys occurred at the height of the species' breeding season!

4
Mississippi Kites and Twentieth-Century Environmental Change

From the history of exploration we glean a rather amazing contrast between the distribution of the Mississippi Kite of yesteryear and its range today—a change that seems "quite without precedent among American birds," as Oberholser phrases it in *The Bird Life of Texas*. Since its first contact with American science, the Mississippi Kite has shifted its primary breeding range out of the baldcypress swamps and the eastern edge of the American prairies—a shift not only remarkable, but also remarkably rapid. It stands in stark contrast to the situation of most birds—the Black-billed Magpie, for instance, which in 15,000 years has been unable to extend its range from the Rocky Mountains to what would seem favorable circumstances farther east. In 1840, Audubon wrote that the Mississippi Kite "confines itself to the borders of deep woods, or those [near] the shores of rivers, lakes or bayous" and "never moves into the interior of the country." Today kites still nest in the country where Custis, Wilson, and Audubon wrote the initial descriptions of the species. But, where nineteenth-century western explorers found few or no Mississippi Kites—the arid Southern High Plains and southwestern deserts—in the late twentieth century kites thrive in large colonies.

Something in the environmental history of the Southwest during the past century apparently has created new possibilities for Mississippi Kites farther west of the country the birds favored when North America was a wilderness. The changes are almost certainly human-caused, and perhaps were set in motion by the clearing of swamplands—no doubt enhanced by indiscriminate shooting—within the birds' traditional range in the late nineteenth century.

Then, between 1910 and 1940, vegetative changes farther west drew both cicada populations and kites into a steady westward movement. The Eurasian exotic shrub saltcedar, introduced by the Department of Agriculture for flood control around 1910, spread rapidly along every river course of the Southern Plains and the Desert Southwest. Grassland fires that had once burned even riparian corridors on the High Plains were suppressed. In the 1930s, as the Dust Bowl raged, the Prairie States Forestry Project employed Civilian Conservation Corps workers to plant more than 218 million trees in shelterbelts along the 98th and 99th meridians. As the rows of trees matured, the shelterbelts created the unexpected windfall of new habitat for wildlife. Another exotic tree, the Siberian elm, became a staple planting for southwestern homesteaders; supplied by county agents, the elms were widely planted in areas where trees had never grown before. Thus, saltcedars, shelterbelts and the emerging groves of Siberian elms drew cicadas—and Mississippi Kites.

As nineteenth-century explorers such as Long and Woodhouse documented so well, colonies of Mississippi Kites occurred along the prairie edges of the Great Plains for thousands of years of Indian occupancy. Then both the numbers and distribution of many species of American wildlife contracted in the shock wave of transformation from Indian to Euroamerican land-use practices. But like coyotes, white-tailed deer, and a few other species that have thrived in the environmental disturbance of contemporary civilization, Mississippi Kites capitalized on a new opportunity when it presented itself. When the despoilers and transformers of the wilderness moved west, the kites hitched a ride.

Breeding and Nesting

Migration

*O*ne of America's first professional ornithologists, Frank M. Chapman, provides us with what may be the best account of Mississippi Kites arriving in the United States from their wintering grounds. His observations occurred in the vicinity of Corpus Christi, Texas.

> This species was first observed April 24, when nine individuals were seen flying northward. The following day we crossed a great flight of these birds. They could be seen to the limit of vision both to the north and south, and about twenty-five were in sight at one time. They flew northward at varying heights; some were within gunshot, while others were so far above the earth that they looked no larger than swallows.

In southern Louisiana, Audubon recorded their arrival "about the middle of April, in small parties of five or six." Farther north, at the edge of their range on the plains, the birds arrive proportionately later: records for 7 May (Oklahoma) and 9 May (Kansas) appear in the literature. Bent cites 1–15 May as the usual period for the arrival of Mississippi Kites in Oklahoma. His report of 1 March for northern Florida seems unusually early and indeed may be suspect. On the High Plains of the Texas Panhandle, near Lubbock, kites normally appear in the skies during the first week of May.

Santa Ana National Wildlife Refuge lies along the Rio Grande near the southern tip of Texas. Its location and brushy habitat—some of the last of its kind amidst a sea of agriculture—makes Santa Ana one of the finest places in North America for observing birds. In a typical spring at Santa Ana, migrating Mississippi Kites are commonplace by 11 April, although biologists Paul Kerlinger and Sidney Gauthreaux report an occasional bird in passage a few days before. Their daily counts of kites showed one to six birds between 2 and 11 April, then a jump to 36 birds the next day. Counts of 15 to 30 birds were recorded on the three days thereafter and none on 16 April. Kites were observed in mixed-species flocks only four times, and of these, Broad-winged Hawks were the usual company for kites. By comparison, Swainson's and Broad-winged hawks flocked together in 24 out of 36 sightings of mixed flocks. The study concluded that Mississippi Kites tend to exhibit strong flocking behavior, a trait consistent with long-distance migration, and they were less likely to migrate in a common flock with other species.

Flocks of migrating Mississippi Kites at times may assume much larger proportions. According to one authority, spring-time flocks as large as 1,500 birds have crossed the Rio Grande at the Santa Ana Refuge. Farther south, in the Veracruz area of the eastern coast of Mexico, as many as 2,371 kites were observed on 27 April and, overall, the count determined that 12,432 kites (with the total estimated at 17,000) passed through the area in the course of the study. Late in the afternoon, often at sunset, the flights settled in two or three large trees—surely representing what must be one of the more spectacular sights in the world of ornithology.

The coastal plains of eastern Mexico are in fact a relatively narrow pathway for migrating kites. Not far to the west rises the Sierra Madre Oriental, whose peaks act as a barrier for kites and other birds that do not normally venture into mountainous habitat. Such a setting forms what is known as a migration corridor. Thus, in season and at a particularly advantageous site, one can observe the migrations of kites and other hawks with considerable ease.

Except for its direction, fall migration for Mississippi Kites is little different from their passage in spring, although the flocks in autumn include young-of-the-year and thus those birds that are undertaking their first migratory trip. The fall flocks include three age groups: adults; yearlings that next year will no longer differ in plumage from adults; and the current year's juveniles.

As in the spring, the migrating flocks in fall also may be sizable. An observer in Oklahoma watched at least 250 kites riding the winds ahead of a rapidly moving storm in early September. Unpublished data collected by Glenn D. Swartz include a flock of more than 2,500 kites observed on 21 September 1990 at Corpus Christi, Texas. At the same location a year later, Swartz recorded flocks of 300 to 700 kites moving southward between mid-August and late September. Along the migration corridor in eastern Mexico, also during the first week of September, 5,130 Mississippi Kites moved southward in the course of a few hours. Farther to the south, in Panama, observers have recorded flights of some 1,000 kites migrating along the Caribbean coastline on 15 October, although at this time and location the flights may include numbers of the look-alike Plumbeous Kite.

Birds migrating to and from South America move along one or more of three major routes: overland, through Mexico and Central America; across the Gulf of Mexico, usually via the Yucatán Peninsula; and an island-hopping route through the Caribbean. The second of these, the trans-Gulf route, is of particular interest since land birds can neither rest nor feed once under way across the vast expanse of open water. Occasionally, large numbers of birds die en route across the Gulf when they encounter adverse weather.

The available information, which we have highlighted here, clearly indicates that Mississippi Kites follow the overland route in migration. That choice agrees with most other species of large-bodied land birds, few of which undertake unbroken flights of great distance (remarkably, many small birds, among them many species of wood warblers, regularly migrate across the Gulf of Mexico). Such birds as the European White Stork, for example, cross the narrow gap between Spain and Morocco or fly well to the east and pass through Israel rather than taking a direct flight across the Mediterranean Sea. For White Storks and many other large land birds, the energy demands of long flights are so costly that they usually preclude migratory routes that lack rest stops. Moreover, many large birds rely on thermals, which do not develop to any great extent over water. Nonetheless, some particularly swift fliers such as Peregrine Falcons may migrate across moderate-sized tracts of water, but headwinds of more than 6 m.p.h. greatly increase the dangers of doing so.

We mention all of this because of the suggestion that a few Mississippi Kites apparently migrate across the Gulf of Mexico, or at least may attempt such a flight. However, supporting evidence is circumstantial and is limited largely to the time when some kites arrive in Florida. That is, the arrival dates for some kites seemingly preclude the birds' having followed the much longer journey overland around the perimeter of the Gulf of Mexico. Other sources suggest that kites apparently head out over the Gulf during their southward migration, but the actual passage of the birds across the Gulf remains unconfirmed.

2
Courtship Behavior

Few details are available regarding the courtship of Mississippi Kites, perhaps because this ritual apparently occurs during the winter months when the birds are still deep in the interior of South America. Courtship behavior is seldom observed on the breeding grounds in North America, although it also may be because the displays are not showy. In any case, and notwithstanding their flocking behavior during migration, pairs seem well formed when the birds arrive in North America. Because the birds often return to previously used nest sites, it has been suggested that the pairs mate for life. At times, pair bonds may be reinforced when the birds soar together and join in mutual swoop displays, but courtship flights of this sort are not commonplace on the breeding grounds.

Copulations occur once the pairs have established their nesting sites. Prior to copulation, the males often present their mates with insects, and from their perches, the females advertise their receptiveness by calling for tokens of food. Occasionally, a female may follow her mate until the food is exchanged. In Illinois, graduate student Sherri Evans noted that copulation typically follows within 10 minutes of an exchange of food and occurs about four times per hour at the peak of mating. She reported an instance where one pair copulated eight times in 2 hours, but she also cited cases where other pairs might mate five or six times in the space of 15 minutes.

3
Nest Locations

It is difficult to describe in any precise way the nesting habitat of Mississippi Kites. Out West, one might begin by looking among the cottonwoods rising from the canyon floors or in the much shorter mesquites dotting the broad plains. In the East, we would focus our searches in riparian forests, those ecologically precious woodlands that border streams and other bodies of water. Late in the last century, biologist C. Hart Merriam listed the Mississippi Kite as a bird typical of the biological zone identified as the Austroriparian Faunal Area in his classic bulletin *Life Zones and Crops Zones of the United States*. In this pioneering treatise on biological regions, Merriam assigned the Gulf and South Atlantic states, excepting the southern third of peninsular Florida, to the Austroriparian Area, a region rich in streamside forests of cypress, tupelo, magnolia, and live oak.

But these are no more than generalities, for kite nests have been found in many settings and in many kinds of trees. In addition to those trees already mentioned, kites also nest in loblolly and shortleaf pine; sweetgum; osage orange; soapberry; locust; hackberry; white, red, shinnery, and blackjack oaks; walnut; willow; and elm. On the plains, the latter is typically the Siberian elm, an exotic species widely used in shelterbelts. Siberian elms have survived because of their greater resistance, compared with American elms, to the fungus causing Dutch elm disease. In central Arizona, Mississippi Kites often nest

Cypress forests bordering the bayous of the southeastern United States are representative of the habitat where naturalist Peter Custis and painters Alexander Wilson and John James Audubon watched Mississippi Kites early in the last century (upper). Westward, far more arid habitat also attracts nesting kites, as illustrated here on the plains of Texas. In recent decades, Mississippi Kites also began nesting in city parks, golf courses, and other urbanized areas. Photos courtesy of Dan Flores.

in pecan orchards, yet another indication of the birds' adaptability.

In recent years, perhaps going back three decades, Mississippi Kites started nesting in urban environments, including college campuses, cemeteries, parks, golf courses, and tree-lined streets in residential areas. This phenomenon is interesting enough to deserve further discussion, which we will do later. But whether in rural or urban settings, trees are not selected as nesting sites because of their species, but rather because their size and structure are suitable for housing a nest. Because only living trees are selected, kite nests usually are well concealed by the foliage that has developed by the time nesting begins.

4
Nests

Unless they meet with unseasonable weather or other adversity, Mississippi Kites normally begin building their nests in early May. Thereafter, most kites begin laying their eggs in the second half of May, extending into mid-June. For Texas, Oklahoma, and Kansas, Bent lists egg dates extending from 15 March to 25 June. However, the validity of the date for March is suspect since the arrival dates at the end of spring migration occur well after mid-March. About half Bent's records are for the period between 3 and 12 June. Based on Parker's extensive study, large numbers of eggs were laid from 10 May to 20 June in nests on the Great Plains. Only one clutch of eggs is laid each year, and ornithologists thus regard the species as single-brooded. However, Mississippi Kites may attempt a second nesting if their first effort is destroyed early in the season.

The size of kite nests is almost as variable as the habitat in which they occur. Some are so small as to belie the size of their owners. But in their external dimensions most nests are 11–14 inches in diameter and 5–7 inches deep. The bowl holding the eggs is shallow (1–2 inches in depth) and about 5 inches in diameter.

The construction appears flimsy, consisting of sticks about the thickness of a pencil or smaller, and at first glance the nest looks like a large version of a Mourning Dove's nest. Despite the shabby external appearance, the lining presents an interesting feature: fresh leaves are added regularly, as often as every day, according to some observers, and the leaves are not necessarily of the same species as the tree supporting the nest. Pecan, sumac, walnut, mesquite, willow, and oak leaves have been noted, but no doubt a complete listing would be much longer. Sutton noted that green twigs of 6 to 8 inches in length are carried to the nest, plucked of their leaves and the defoliated stem shoved aside. At least one nest in Texas was recorded as lined with "green moss" and another in Louisiana with "Spanish moss."

The function of the leafy lining remains obscure, but it may concern sanitary conditions in the nest. The lining forms a protective covering over decaying remains of food, thereby keeping young kites somewhat apart from such debris and the vermin it might attract. A. S. Jackson believes that the fresh leaves act as a "kind of air conditioning" in the heat of a southern summer, and others suggest shading as a function. This nest-lining habit occurs in many other birds of prey throughout the world, including 17 other species of North American falconiformes, but some gather grasses or reeds instead of leaves. Despite such widespread occurrence of the behavior, however, a sound theory for its significance is not at hand. Raptor authorities Leslie Brown and Dean Amadon suggest that greenery provides some kind of an "emotional" (their word) experience, perhaps supplanting the hunting instinct in females, thereby keeping them in the vicinity of the nest so that the young are not left unguarded.

At times Mississippi Kites may use nests previously constructed by other species of birds. A. C. Bent said that old crow's nests "may be appropriated." More commonly, however, kites will reuse their own old nests. In some years, 30 to 50 percent of the nests may be those used for a second or third year, and one of Bent's sources indicated that a pair of kites used the same nest for 5 years. However, kite nests, even when

[40]

reused, do not steadily increase in size via yearly accumulation of materials. In contrast, the nests of some other raptors may reach sizable proportions when an abundance of new materials are added over the course of several years—a Bald Eagle's nest in Florida extended to a depth of more than 20 feet, and a Sea Eagle's nest in Europe weighed 2 tons. After many years of observations in Texas, Jackson concluded that the first evidence for the reuse of last year's nest is the appearance each morning of a fresh lining of green leaves.

At a wildlife center in South Carolina, a pair of Swallow-tailed Kites once selected a year-old Mississippi Kite nest. The swallowtails simply refurbished the nest with Spanish moss and some twigs and set up shop. Interestingly, there was no evidence during a 5-year period that Swallow-tailed Kites used their own nests a second time, even though at least six nests (of 28) likely were built by the same pairs of birds returning to the same site in 2 consecutive years. In this area of coastal South Carolina, Swallow-tailed Kites and Mississippi Kites usually nest in similar habitat (pine forests and riparian woodlands), and both typically select sites in tall loblolly pines. Moreover, as Audubon observed in 1821, the two species of kites often mix together when feeding.

Reuse of the same nest implies that at least some, if not all, kites may return each year to the same nesting area, a behavioral pattern known as migrational homing. The evidence currently available for Mississippi Kites is only circumstantial, but the notion gains support from fieldwork in Arizona, where three nestlings were banded and seen the following year less than 2 miles from where they were banded. A suggestion of the tenacity associated with homing behavior is found in the record of a kite originally banded in Louisiana in 1979 and recovered in 1987 at exactly the same latitude and longitude after an interlude of eight round trips to the wintering grounds. Still, conclusive proof will require individually marking a number of nesting adults and their offspring and then finding those birds actually breeding at the same locale in subsequent years, a task made more difficult by the necessary commitment to long-term fieldwork and the inescapable fact that mortality will steadily diminish the size of the sample.

For Mississippi Kites, nest building is not the feverish activity associated with some birds, but is instead a leisurely process that may take well over a week to complete. Kites under close observation added fewer than a half dozen twigs in a morning's work, although the pace may be more rapid later in the season. Even when refurbishing a previously used nest, which after a year's neglect may be a ramshackle structure, the kites go about their task without evidence of hurry. A pair may linger nearby for days without adding a single twig to the old nest.

Most of the nest materials are gathered from living vegetation rather than as dead twigs and sticks. Sutton watched a male (he identified males on the basis of their "clear white" head plumage) snip a leaf-covered twig from a locust tree and carry the sprig in its bill to a nearby nest where the twig was shaken, dropped, and picked up repeatedly in what Sutton called "fussing." The female, perched nearby, then flew to the ground, picked up a twig with one foot, and added it to the nest. In another account, one of Bent's sources wrote that a soaring kite suddenly dropped "swift as an arrow down through the trees and reappeared [overhead] with an oak twig in his talons," then wheeled and flew to its rudimentary nest in a gum tree. Moreover, "both birds worked, darting in among the trees as on the first occasion, and reappearing with either a twig or spray of green leaves. At last, as the midday hour began to cast short shadows," the birds perched and work ceased.

Most nests are situated in the upper branches of whatever trees are selected, but their actual height above ground varies in keeping with the available vegetation. Thus, nests may be positioned at almost any height above ground—quite high in some cases, much less so in others. In some settings, the nests may be surprisingly low. In the shinnery oak country of Oklahoma, for example, Sutton described kite nests only 5–6 feet above ground and remarked how "thrilling it was to look *down* [his emphasis] at the incubating birds from horseback." Kite nests constructed in low-growing mesquites in some parts of

Nest and eggs of a Mississippi Kite. Note the fresh leaves lining the nest's interior, a variously explained feature of several species of raptors. The clutch almost always consists of two eggs, although one and sometimes three eggs have been reported (see text). Eggs are bluish white. Photo courtesy of Wyman P. Meinzer.

Texas are often only 4–6 feet above ground. At the other extreme, Bent reported nests at heights of 60, 80, 111, 119, and 135 feet above ground.

5
Neighbors

Other species of animals often share the area immediately surrounding the nests of Mississippi Kites. These include wasps and small birds, which often nest mere inches away from the larger kites. In one instance observed by James W. Parker, wasps built their nest on the underside of a kite's nest, and at another site, the wasps traveled on the limbs next to the nest. The kite nests produced young in each case, and in both cases, there was no evidence that the kites fed on the readily available wasps.

On two occasions, House Sparrows also had the temerity to build their nests on the underside of kite nests. Blue Jays, Mourning Doves, Northern Mockingbirds, and Brown Thrashers are among the other birds nesting near Mississippi Kites. Parker related two curious anecdotes concerning these neighbors. In one case, a small kite nestling apparently fell from its own nest and landed in the nest of a Brown Thrasher, and the thrasher was apparently caring for the misplaced kite! In the other, Mockingbirds and Mississippi Kites nesting in the same tree at times joined forces and together vigorously defended their nesting area against intruders.

6
Clutch Size and Description of Eggs

The completed clutches of Mississippi Kites, as often reported, may consist of one, two, or, rarely, three eggs. A clutch of two eggs, however, is by far the most common. In Oklahoma, 40 nests watched by the well-known ornithologist George M. Sutton included 38 with two eggs and two with one egg each.

Reports of three-egg clutches seem suspect in light of thorough studies by James W. Parker. His fieldwork uncovered no instances of three-egg clutches in the 457 nests he examined, nor, as reported by A. S. Jackson, did any occur in a sample of more than 1,000 nests observed in the early 1900s near Vernon, Texas. In the deep South, A. F. Ganier found three-egg clutches just three times in 500 nests studied in Mississippi. Parker attributes the reports of three-egg clutches primarily to a few observations of three fledglings, which more than likely had hatched in separate nests in the same clump of trees. He also believes that clutches of one egg actually represent instances of a two-egg clutch from which one egg had been lost (which must occur rather often, given that in some years almost half of the nests he observed contained a single egg).

On the other hand, the majority (64 percent) of nests studied in Illinois contained but one egg, thus suggesting to Sherri Evans that regional differences in food supplies might dictate clutch size. Food availability does influence the clutch sizes in some species of raptors, with fewer eggs produced when food is not abundant. For Barn Owls, year-to-year adjustments in clutch size correlate with the abundance of mice on which the adults feed their young—an obvious adaptation to avoid having too many mouths to feed in hard times. Based on her data, Evans concluded that kites nesting in southern Illinois, at the northern edge of their breeding range, may in fact experience food shortages and therefore commonly produce one-egg clutches. She cited poor hatching success for nests with two-egg clutches as further evidence that food was limited at her study area.

There the matter rests—one- or two-egg clutches, perhaps depending on food availability—again indicating the desirability for further research.

The eggs are smooth, blueish white, and normally unmarked, but the shells often become stained during incubation. Some eggs may show faint pale brown spots, but pigmented markings are rare. It seems likely, as Charles Bendire suspected long ago, that stains on the eggs result from contact with the decaying green leaves lining the nests. Other species of kites nesting in the United States have eggs well marked with irregular spots and splashes of brown, chestnut brown, or umber.

In shape the eggs of Mississippi Kites are somewhat variable, ranging from nearly oval to rounded ovate, and average 1.6 by 1.3 inches in size. There was a time when some colonies of kites suffered at the hands of egg collectors. However, egg collecting (oology), once a popular hobby and the basis of extensive private collections, is no longer legal, and legitimate scientific needs for the eggs of wild birds are now governed by strict state and federal regulations.

7
Incubation

In Mississippi Kites, both sexes share incubation duties, but until a number of breeding adults are caught, individually marked, and carefully observed, the actual contribution of each parent to incubation cannot be determined. Nor will we learn much about the pattern, if any, of the daily cycle. In Mourning Doves, for example, females incubate at night, whereas males tend the eggs during the day. Moreover, the exchange of shifts at the nest in some species of birds is accompanied by ritualistic behavior. Except for the possibility that the arriving mate brings a leafy twig as a ceremonial offering, the subject of incubation changeover in Mississippi Kites is yet another topic awaiting detailed study.

Assuming that shared incubation means that there are no lapses in attendance, one can suggest two advantages: assurance of continuous, regulated temperature for the developing embryos (blankets of down are not present in kite nests) and a round-the-clock alert to egg predators. Incubation begins with the laying of the first egg and continues for the following 29–31 days.

8
Nest Fates and Defense

Weather and predators are the most serious threats to the nests of Mississippi Kites. Hail badly damaged seven nests in the timber bordering the Medicine River in Kansas; one of these was smashed to the ground. Presumably, any of the violent storms that arise on the plains might badly damage kite nests despite the close attention of a dutiful parent. Sutton suspected that fox squirrels, whatever their motive, destroyed a nest in Oklahoma.

Predators of kite eggs include crows, ravens, jays, and raccoons. Nestling kites likely fall prey to owls and some of the larger raptors such as Swainson's Hawks. Tree-climbing snakes such as rat snakes, most of which relish eggs and young birds, also are probable threats in some areas. Mississippi Kites vigorously attack such intruders, but their assault usually is more show than substance and little harm generally befalls predators of their eggs or young. Such aggressive displays often involve several birds. Besides the parents, virtually all kites in the immediate area, once alerted, may join in the harassment of intruders. James W. Parker asserts that Great Horned Owls elicit the most intense response of any predator, and they also are more likely to suffer an actual strike from the diving kites. He reported the demise of an entire colony of kites in Texas when a Great Horned Owl steadily destroyed the nests one by one during a 2-week period. And, in some areas of prairie country, owls may appear in one out of four shelterbelts. In reality, if the showy attack fails to dissuade a predator, a Mississippi Kite's nest remains about as vulnerable to predation as the eggs or nestlings of any other bird. Parker also found that ants at times plagued newly hatched nestlings, thereby contributing to the complete or partial failure of three nests in Oklahoma. Overall, however, ants were judged a minor cause of nest failure in his study of more than 400 kite nests, and they seem critical only when very young kites are attacked en masse.

9
Territoriality and Colonial Nesting

The term *territory* has been variously defined, but we will stick with a simple yet efficient definition: a defended area. Implicit in this definition is that the defended area is associated with courtship and breeding behavior.

As noted, Mississippi Kites vigorously attack intruders, but such behavior is not evidence of intraspecific territoriality, and indeed the Mississippi Kite is not a species that defends a site against others of its own kind. In fact, kites are just the opposite; they are highly social and often nest in what some biologists call "colonies."

Hence, what is territoriality and how does it differ from the attack behavior often so evident in Mississippi Kites? Much has been written on the topic, but we will be brief. Many birds, most commonly males in courtship, defend a specific site with highly ritualized behavior, usually with displays of plumage and/or calls and songs. And the defended area very often is not a site of any inherent value such as a food source or a nest location. The drumming behavior of a Ruffed Grouse is a good example: the drumming site, a log or stump, is of no immediate value, but to the cock grouse it is "his and his alone." The territorial behavior of males sends two messages, one to other males ("keep away") and the other to winsome females ("I am here and looking for a mate"). Most important, territorial behavior is directed toward others of the same species. Thus, territorial behavior is associated with courtship, and it is quite different from the attacks that kites employ when their nests or young are threatened by unwelcome intruders.

Mississippi Kites at times nest in close proximity to each other, forming what are often called "colonies," although some biologists are more restrictive in their use of the term. One observer located more than 40 nests in the cottonwoods at Meade State Park in Kansas and believed he may have overlooked as many more. Not to be outdone, Texas produced an even larger colony of about 100 nests on a 40-acre site, including some trees with more than one nest. We once discovered two active nests in the same tree, a Siberian elm on the corner of a busy street in Lubbock, Texas.

Shelterbelts apparently foster colonial nesting. These strips of trees often provide habitat for four to six kite nests, but the largest colony thus far reported in a single shelterbelt consisted of 15 nests. Kite nests in shelterbelts are spaced about 125 yards apart, but sometimes as close as 14 yards, although some shelterbelts, for reasons that are not apparent, lack nests altogether. In reporting these data, Parker noted that fewer than 10 percent of the nests he studied on the Great Plains were solitary. In some locations such as riparian forests, colonial nesting is not as apparent.

The social nature of Mississippi Kites is also evident in their habit of roosting together, sometimes in large numbers. One September an ornithologist observed a communal roost in Kansas that included at least 200 birds. We have not had the delight of witnessing a gathering of the same magnitude, but such pre-migration gatherings must be common, for in early September we have seen up to 15 kites assembled in a single dead hackberry tree in Texas. On several June mornings in the same area we watched a daily congregation of six kites in trees bordering a trickle of a stream. The birds perched amicably, sometimes three to a tree, and on occasion two or more dropped to the streamside. Never on these or any other occasions have we observed behavior that might indicate territoriality or, indeed, any other sort of aggression.

Nestling Mississippi Kites. Note that one nestling is somewhat larger than the other, the result of asynchronous hatching typical of raptors. In times of food shortages, only the larger bird survives, nature's way of insuring the survival of at least one of the young birds. Photo courtesy of Wyman P. Meinzer.

Raising Young

I
Hatching

Two conditions are important in the microcosm of a kite nest: first, that the two eggs are not laid the same day, and second, that incubation nonetheless begins when the first egg is laid. Thus, the two eggs do not hatch at the same time— James W. Parker recorded an average interval of about 4 days— and one chick therefore has a headstart and gains size-related dominance over its younger sibling.

The generally accepted explanation for asynchronous hatching, which is not unusual among birds of prey, considers the availability of food and the assurance that at least some of the nestlings survive in times of scarcity. In other words, if the supply of prey is limited—and it often may be—the first-hatched youngsters gain a competitive advantage over their smaller nest mates and monopolize the food brought to the nest. Despite the temptation to do so, we should not assign the parents any humanistic sense of fair play regarding their nestlings. Natural selection, not morality, governs nature. And in hard times, the parent birds contribute to this template of survival by favoring the larger nestlings with their deliveries of food.

This setting—nestlings of different sizes and their rivalry for food—raises another spectre of nature's relentless quest for genetic preservation. In times of privation, birds of prey may thwart starvation when the larger nestlings kill and feed on their smaller siblings. Again, nature's austere ways are designed to assure that some part of the brood survives during hard times; otherwise, all would starve. Cannibalism is difficult to document and, in fact, probably is quite rare in Mississippi Kites. No doubt their insectivorous diet lessens its occurrence. Nonetheless, kite nestlings do sometimes disappear without a trace, and while there could be other explanations for these disappearances, the possibility remains that nestling kites at times may practice cannibalism as a draconian form of "survival of the fittest."

2
Parental Care of Nestlings

As with incubation, both parents attend the nestlings with round-the-clock devotion. Again, there are few detailed studies (often known as *time budgets*) about the degree to which each parent contributes to these responsibilities, although there are indications that females may spend more time than males at the nest with their broods. Both parents engage in hunting and delivering food, although males apparently provide somewhat more of the nestlings' fare than females. The parent birds usually forage near their nests during this demanding period of the birds' breeding cycle.

So far as can be determined—the circumstances are understandably difficult to ascertain—food brought to the nestlings does not vary significantly from the diet of the adults. As might be expected, however, newly hatched kites are fed materials softened in the esophagus of their parents, then regurgitated at the nest.

The adults' behavior changes somewhat as their offspring mature in the nest. At first, while the nestlings are all mouth and still fully cloaked in downy plumage, the parents disgorge food en masse, from which a piece at a time is picked up and placed in the mouth of a nestling. Later, the nestlings themselves pick at the disgorged food without further aid from their parents. Still later, bits of dismembered prey are gradually substituted for the diet of partially digested food. Regurgitated food is no longer offered by the time the nestlings are 11 days old.

A few observations are available regarding the frequency with which young kites are fed by their parents. In one study, nestlings of unspecified age were fed on average about once every 11 minutes. In another investigation, the parents fed newly hatched kites three times per hour, increasing to three to five times per hour by the time the nestlings were 10 days old. The parents don't linger when delivering food. The average visit lasts just 51 seconds, and if the few cases of longer visits (up to 4 minutes) are omitted, the average falls to no more than 30 seconds. These data suggest the intensity and demands associated with day-to-day parental care. Moreover, the food-providing abilities of adult kites was highlighted when a biologist experimentally placed "extra" young in a few nests, with the result that the extended families—now numbering three or even four nestlings—were raised without evidence of privation.

Scraps of leftover food sometimes remain in kite nests, offering clues about the diet of the nestlings. Of course, such evidence fails to indicate those foods that are completely consumed, so there is a bias that favors detection of those foods that are not entirely palatable. Along with the rear legs of grasshoppers, the remains at one nest included the rear legs of leopard frogs as well as the hard wing covers of beetles, part of a dragonfly, and the decapitated body of a bullfrog.

At times food falls from kite nests, becoming a resource that may influence the food habits of an unlikely associate of Mississippi Kites. James W. Parker discovered an ornate box turtle foraging on scraps of large insects and small vertebrates under a kite nest in a shelterbelt in Oklahoma. Because box turtles have localized, heavily traveled home ranges and a strong tendency to revisit their feeding areas, Parker suggests that a beneficial affiliation might be developing between the soaring kite and the lowly turtle! The potential for such a relationship is enhanced on the Great Plains, where kites often place their nests relatively low to the ground, thereby increasing the concentration of dropped food beneath nest-bearing vegetation (i.e., scraps falling from greater heights generally scatter over a larger area on the ground). Interestingly, the breeding range of the Mississippi Kite virtually overlaps the entire distribution of box turtles (two species) occurring in the United States.

3
Fledglings

At hatching, juvenile kites are feeble and unable to hold their heads erect for more than a few moments at a time. According to some reports, they also lack motor skills in their feet and legs, so that in the earliest stages of development the nestlings support themselves upright on outer parts of their underpinnings. Despite this awkwardness, the nestlings are attractive and clothed in a fluff of white down. Sutton, with an artist's eye for color, describes a newly hatched kite as follows:

> It was a lovely creature, its down pure white with a small, faint area of buffy brown on the nape and a wash of the same pale brown over the back and upper surface of the wings. The region in front of and about the eyes was dull gray, the marking occupying almost precisely the same position as the black facial mask of the adult. The bill was dull blue-gray, the cere dull brownish-orange, the corners of the mouth light orange. The feet were pale, clear yellow-orange with gray claws. The eyes were dull gray-brown, with bluish pupils; the eyelids dull gray.

4
Helpers

Some birds have evolved a curious social system associated with breeding activities. Nonbreeding birds share in the care of the offspring, sometimes including incubation and, more commonly, feeding of the nestlings. Ornithologists have dubbed these extraparental birds as "helpers-at-the-nest," and Mississippi Kites are among the species that employ, at least to some degree, this interesting practice.

Helpers often have some genetic relationship with the parents, perhaps as siblings or as earlier offspring, and therefore are also genetically related to some extent with the young in the current nest. In these cases, biologists have advanced "kin selection" as the explanation for the existence of helpers. Kin selection proposes that it is to the advantage of the helpers to ensure the successful rearing of the nestlings by helping the parents. The process enhances the survival of individuals with at least some of the same genes as the helpers, thereby continuing a common genetic lineage of all concerned. Just why the helpers themselves do not breed is not always clear, but it may be that the environment does not contain enough resources to support additional nests, so that some birds become helpers instead of breeders. Other scenarios for helping undoubtedly occur among birds.

Helping behavior is rare in raptors, although Galapagos Hawks and Harris Hawks (the latter is a species of the southwestern United States) exhibit a type of helping in which several males assist in the care of a single nest. In Mississippi Kites, the phenomenon of helping has not been thoroughly studied, and much remains uncertain about the relationships, both genetic and ecological, that may be involved. So far as is presently known, the helpers are yearlings—those kites between 12 and 24 months old—and still showing barred tail feathers as a remnant of juvenile plumage. The activities of the helpers observed by James W. Parker and others include assistance with nest construction, incubation, brooding, and, most often, nest defense against predators. However, helpers do not necessarily, or even regularly, make all of these contributions. In San Angelo, Texas, yearling kites were present at more than half of the 22 nests under observation, and their participation was limited, so far as was determined, to defending the nests against intruders.

In a larger sample of 209 nests, yearlings accompanied mated pairs of kites on 35 (17 percent) occasions, but conclusive data were obtained for only a few of these observations. Nonetheless, on two occasions yearlings shared incubation duties with a pair of adults. In one case, the helper sat for about 15 percent of the total time that incubation was observed. In the other instance, a yearling attended a nest containing an egg and a newly hatched nestling. Helping was suspected at 15 other nests, but assistance with incubation was not confirmed in these instances. In one of these nests, two helpers were involved.

For the present, we can conclude that nest defense by yearlings is the most common form of helping in Mississippi Kites. Presumably, these efforts increase nest success, as they do for Harris Hawks. In turn, helpers-at-the-nest profit from their association with breeding adults by gaining valuable experience for their own nesting efforts in subsequent years.

5
Reproductive Success

Ornithologists express the year-to-year success of the nesting season in various terms. Common among these are
   (a) the percentage of nests that produce at least one fledgling (reciting the percentage of nests in which eggs simply hatch, while of some interest, does not necessarily influence the next generation, since young in the nest might die before fledging);
   (b) the average number of young fledged per successful nest; and finally,
   (c) the average number of young fledged per nesting attempt.
Based on a large-scale study that included the fates of 391 kite nests in Kansas, Oklahoma, and Texas, James W. Parker reported that 49 percent of the nests hatched at least one egg, with an average of 1.29 young fledged per successful nest. When all nests, both successful and unsuccessful were included, the average dropped to 0.63 young per nesting attempt. In Arizona, at the western edge of the species' distribution in North America, the results were almost identical: 34 of 63 nests (54 percent) successfully fledged 44 young kites during a 4-year period. The average was about 1.3 young per successful nest and 0.60 young fledged per nesting attempt. In another study, this one of 28 nests in southern Illinois on the northern edge of the breeding range, 61 percent of the nests were successful, all nests produced an average of about 0.6 young, and in each successful nest, a single young kite reached flying age.

Thus, across a large area of their breeding range, Mississippi Kites show a remarkable similarity in nesting success and production, as summarized in Table 1.

Table 1

Location	Number Nests	% Hatching	Number Young Produced	
			Per Nest	Per Successful Nest
Great Plains	391	49	0.63	1.29
Arizona	63	54	0.60	1.29
Illinois	28	61	0.61	1.00

Surprisingly, studies of similar scope have not been conducted in the southern heartland—from Louisiana to South Carolina—of the species's range. We must assume that the estimates from the other areas of North America also reflect the production of kites in a rather dissimilar environment in the eastern half of the continent. From the data at hand, we can generalize in the following way. For every 100 nesting attempts, about half of the nests will hatch at least one egg, and from these 60 young birds will survive to flying age. Stated another way, 200 breeding birds (100 pairs) produce 60 young each year, so that 23 percent (60/260) of the post-breeding population consists of young birds, which in a steady-state population also means that 23 percent of the entire population dies every year. In the latter scenario, births equal deaths, which gives a population ecologist a crude way of determining mortality rates, if we assume that a population is neither increasing or decreasing. In the case at hand, the matter is further complicated by the presence of yearlings, only some of which may breed.

Reproductive success may be much greater in special environments. In a municipal park in New Mexico, which included a golf course and zoo, biologist Antonio L. Gennaro recorded an average of nearly 1.2 fledglings per nesting attempt, or about double the production observed elsewhere. He related the high rate of success to a lower incidence of nest predation. The density of trees in many parks and golf courses also may provide kite nests with better-than-normal protection from prairie storms. If this situation continues, as likely may be the case, then urban kite populations may increase more rapidly than their rural counterparts.

Because Mississippi Kites often nest in "colonies," the question arises if colonial nesting is a life-history feature that might increase nesting success. Colonial nesting in such birds as gulls and terns, among many other species, apparently offers the advantage of increased protection from predators. However, neither the Arizona nor the Great Plains studies showed any indication that the close association of kite nests improves production. In fact, Parker determined that isolated pairs of kites actually raise more young per nest than those breeding in colonies. For now, we must conclude that colonial nesting, as it relates to kites, is somehow aligned more with social organization than with a direct influence on improved reproductive success.

Food and Feeding

Feeding Ecology

A summer mirage dances over the Southern Plains, its shimmer producing in our mind's eye a vision of the grassy wilderness of yesteryear. Before us is a cropped lawn of native grasses, green with the rains of early summer and dotted by cloud shadows clear to the curve of the earth. A Chihuahuan Raven preens atop a scrubby oak. Nearby a pair of gray wolves idly scratch their necks. The lean predators reflect on a dozen pronghorns browsing a quarter mile upwind, but the lobos continue their attentions to the troublesome fleas. Prairie dogs bob and chirp, then scurry at the silent shadow of a Golden Eagle. The prairie is wondrous and alive.

But there is more in our vision. From their resting spot in a grove of cottonwoods, whose leaves turn and wink sunlight in the summer breeze, a small herd of bison cows and their red-coated calves emerges. The bison climb from the bottoms along a tepid creek to the undulating plains above, and with their rumbling passage, clouds of insects billow into the air. As if by alchemy, as if the cottonwood leaves had been transformed into birds, sleek, gray-bodied hawks appear, wheeling and sweeping into the buzzing insects.

The Paleolithic hunters who hurled their finely flaked spear points into the ribs of giant bison 9,000 years ago must have witnessed just such scenes as this. Perhaps even the flinty, mercenary hide hunters of the great buffalo slaughter of the last century took notice of the partnership between the bison they shot and the curious gray hawks that circled the herds. But unless the future restores a vast grassland park on the Southern Plains, we will experience such scenes only in those fleeting moments when a mirage once more inspires our imaginations. Except for the kites and the insects, most of the other actors are gone.

As suggested in the foregoing scene, mice and other small vertebrates are not the mainstay in the diet of Mississippi Kites. More than any other prey, large-bodied insects form the usual bulk of their diet, and of these, grasshoppers and cicadas are especially prominent. Beetles, crickets, and dragonflies also are among their varied fare of insects.

Along with owls and other hawks, kites dispose of invertebrate exoskeletons and other undigestible parts of their prey by regurgitating (or "casting") these elements in neatly formed pellets. Such pellets provide biologists with a ready means of determining the diet of birds of prey, although there are biases to consider when using this or any other analysis of food habits. The jawbones and hair of mice in owl pellets, for instance, are relatively easy to associate with a particular species, but other materials may be more difficult to identify. In Oklahoma, noted ornithologist George M. Sutton watched Mississippi Kites cast up pellets of "reddish brown cricket legs," but he could not refine his analysis with more detail.

Mississippi Kites usually disgorge their pellets early in the morning, before the birds leave their nighttime roosts. Henry S. Fitch, who studied kites in Kansas, described the pellets as elliptical, about 15 millimeters in diameter and 30 millimeters in length (or slightly more than 0.5 × 1.0 inches). The pellets he examined were cast with a pink or purplish hue, although we suspect the color probably varies depending on the contents. A large number (205) of pellets cast at Fitch's study area further revealed the dominance of insect foods: beetle and grasshopper remains were common. Three pellets contained what seemed to be shreds of mammal hairs, but save for these, the sample contained no evidence of vertebrates despite the availability of mice, birds, reptiles, and amphibians in the immediate vicinity.

Compared with pellet examinations, the direct analysis of gullet and stomach contents provides a somewhat more exacting dietary analysis. Foods, especially those of soft texture, removed from these organs often may be identified before digestion has destroyed key features. The principal limitation, of course, is that living creatures, including Mississippi Kites, don't readily submit to the indignities resulting from this brand of science. This technique necessarily requires killing a number of birds, some of which may have empty stomachs and thus yield no information to justify their loss. Nonetheless, the stomachs ("gizzards") of 16 Mississippi Kites collected in Oklahoma during May and June revealed a rich assemblage of insect foods: several kinds of beetles (including weevils and ground, scrub, tiger, dung, and wood-boring beetles), crickets, grasshoppers, two kinds of wasps, spiders, some flies, stinkbugs, and moths. Cave (or camel) crickets also occurred in nearly all of the stomachs in this sample. Once again, this study revealed no evidence of mice, birds, or other vertebrates save for the intriguing exception of a single bone from an unidentifiable species of fish.

Cicadas—sometimes erroneously called "locusts"—are a seasonally important food, and the sight of kites in graceful pursuit of these noisy insects often figures in the narratives of nineteenth-century naturalists. Alexander Wilson, for example, observed kites near Natchez, Mississippi, "sweeping about among the trees like Swallows" in search of swarming cicadas, and Stephen Long noted "great numbers of . . . Falco Mississippiensis of Wilson" feeding on cicadas along the course of the Canadian River in Oklahoma.

In some years, immense numbers of cicadas may be available as prey for kites. One recent estimate indicated that 250,000 adult cicadas emerge per 40 hectares (100 acres) of riparian habitat in Arizona each week during the summer, reaching a peak of nearly 700,000 at the height of the season. With such an abundance of food available during the nesting season, it is not surprising that cicadas formed 71 percent of the food Mississippi Kites delivered to their nest-bound offspring in Arizona.

In Texas, the summer of 1991 was just such a peak year for cicadas on the Southern High Plains near Lubbock. No need for scientific measurements—just drive across the Llano Estacado and at every grove of elms or cottonwoods hear the raspy buzz of cicada song drown out ordinary road noise. The kites

Cicadas form a major item in the diet of Mississippi Kites. Several species, including one that emerges after 17 years in the ground, occur in the United States. In Arizona, Mississippi Kites occur in riparian habitat where large numbers of Apache cicada thrive during the summer months. The cast skins of cicada larvae clinging to the surface of tree trunks and limbs are a familiar icon of summer. Photo courtesy of Jack Dermid.

concentrated almost all of their hunting efforts above these groves, each well stocked with hordes of the noisy insects. On several occasions we watched the birds circle a particular grove for 3 or 4 minutes, then chart a straight course across the grasslands to another grove several hundred yards distant. In between, the kites ignored a bumper crop of grasshoppers and instead sought only the cicadas, and they knew exactly where to hunt.

Mississippi Kites are so fond of cicadas that fun-loving ornithologists have on occasion gathered the thick-bodied insects and tossed them one at a time, like peanuts, to birds circling overhead waiting for handouts. Such behavior perhaps develops when and where kites take advantage of human activities that scare cicadas and other insects into the air, thereby associating humans with food. A. C. Bent, whose books about North American birds stand as classics, noted that up to twenty kites "will sail about a person, a horseman or a team, traveling through grassy flats or bushy places, and seize the cicadas as they are scared up."

Black Kites, an abundant and widely distributed species elsewhere in the world, also relish cicadas, and irruptions of the raucous insects apparently attract birds from a wide area. In Australia, an observer watched a flock of more than 135 Black Kites preying on cicadas caught in an updraft along the face of a cliff. On windless days when the updraft dissipated, the kites scattered and fed elsewhere. A somewhat similar event was reported in Florida near the Suwannee River. There hundreds of kites, including both Mississippi and Swallow-tailed kites, feasted for several days on a swarm of grasshoppers of incalculable numbers.

The accepted wisdom in the past was that small birds were not included in the diet of Mississippi Kites. At least one naturalist has reported that such species as Northern Orioles nest in the same trees as kites, and we have seen Red-winged Blackbirds calmly perched within a few feet of an alert kite. In some places, however, perhaps because changes in the American landscape have altered the availability of their prey, Mississippi

Kites today may feed somewhat more on birds than before. Cliff Swallows, for example, readily build their bulbous mud nests under highway bridges, often at sites far removed from natural cliffs, thereby significantly extending the range of these small birds into habitats where they then become available to kites.

Shelterbelts, planted in the 1930s as a consequence of the ruinous Dust Bowl, also have influenced the diet of Mississippi Kites on the southern plains of North America. These strips of trees attracted woodland species of songbirds into the range— and diet—of Mississippi Kites. But any idea that kites or other raptors might be shot or persecuted because of their predation of songbirds has rightly become another Edsel of outdoor lore. In fact, only a few species of raptors, particularly the Coopers Hawk and other accipiters, regularly feed on birds. And accipiters are difficult to find, let alone shoot. Tragically, persons shooting hawks almost always kill those of a far more visible group known as buteos, those thick-bodied hawks with broad wings and fan-shaped tails. Red-tailed Hawks and other buteos, instead of eating songbirds, are actually keen predators of mice—a classic case of mistaken identity! Moreover, the growing appreciation and knowledge of biotic communities has finally made notions of predator control both aesthetically unfashionable and scientifically obsolete. But the uninitiated should note that hawks of all kinds enjoy the full protection of federal law.

John James Audubon, in his journal for 1826, mentioned "a Mississippi Kite devouring the Red-throated lizards" and again, in his renowned *Birds of America*, described the seizure of a "red-throated panting lizard" from a tree top. Audubon probably was referring in both cases to the Carolina (or green) anole, the males of which develop a conspicuous pink dewlap, or throat-fan, during the breeding season. Carolina anoles regularly forage high in trees and occur throughout much of the range of Mississippi Kites in the Southeast.

In Arizona, careful study of more than 2,600 food items carried to three kite nests revealed that vertebrates made up 11 percent of the prey. These included toads, frogs, and a small species of bat known as the western pipistrelle. Pipistrelles are active prior to sundown, and while their flight is erratic, they are not swift fliers. One pair of kites in fact delivered 54 pipistrelles to their nestlings. Overall, however, bats made up less than 2 percent of the foods enumerated in the Arizona study.

Still another means of learning more about the diet of raptors is to examine their nests for the remains of food. Bones and other debris also can be found on the ground beneath kite nests. Using this approach, naturalists have added chimney swifts, ground squirrels, kangaroo rats, deer mice, horned lizards, box turtles and rabbits to the list of foods consumed by Mississippi Kites. Many of these foods, of course, are not available throughout the kite's range and therefore represent regional variations in their diets. Because some food items (e.g., box turtles and rabbits) are almost certainly derived from road kills, we point out that Mississippi Kites and many other predators are also scavengers. Predation as a way of life is, in the "real world," so uncertain that few species of predators ignore the fortuitous availability of carrion. Hence, from an ecological view, there are important distinctions to be made when considering the evidence used to determine how meat-eating animals obtain their food. The only safe conclusion, upon finding a rabbit bone in a kite nest, is to infer that kites will *eat* rabbits, but not necessarily that the birds actually *kill* rabbits. A scenario for the latter seems so unlikely that a rabbit bone should not become evidence of predation until someone offers reliable observations to the contrary.

Food habits form an important component of any species' natural history. As a case in point, food habits seem related to the wintering areas of raptors. Hawks that feed on warm-blooded prey may spend the winter in relatively cold climates, whereas those feeding on cold-blooded prey typically overwinter in much warmer regions. We thus find Rough-legged Hawks, whose diet is dominated by rodents, wintering throughout north-temperate North America. Conversely, the insect-eating Mississippi Kites, as noted earlier, withdraw far to the south where their prey will remain active and available during the winter months. Such a relationship is known for raptors breeding in Europe as well as in North America.

But a knowledge of food habits also helps us understand how humans may influence the ecological health of animals. For example, certain kinds of pesticides—DDT is the most infamous, but there are many others—accumulate in the foods of some birds of prey and, after ingestion, chemically alter the normal production of eggshells. Eggs thus affected have abnormally thin shells that crush during incubation. Populations of such raptors as Bald Eagles and Peregrine Falcons fell precipitously during the decades when DDT was used widely, and both birds remain on the list of endangered species despite the current ban on DDT and related chemicals.

Because these pesticides were designed to control insects, one might assume that Mississippi Kites were similarly afflicted with thinned eggshells. Fortunately, this was not the case, and for a very simple reason: the food chain ending with Mississippi Kites is short enough (plant to insect to kite) that relatively small doses of pesticides reach the birds. In contrast, Bald Eagles stand atop a much longer food chain in an aquatic ecosystem (plants and phytoplankton to zooplankton to insect to minnow to large fish to eagle) in which pesticides accumulate in ever-greater concentrations at each additional link—a process known as biomagnification. Regrettably, DDT and its sister compounds are still being manufactured in America for use elsewhere, particularly in Third World nations. As long as this situation continues, environmental contamination will affect biological life over much of the globe.

We can conclude that Mississippi Kites, while not strictly insectivorous, clearly rely heavily on insect foods for the bulk of their diet. Nonetheless, kites today may rely somewhat more on vertebrates than in earlier times, evidently because of changed habitat conditions in the twentieth century. Moreover, with a diet that sometimes may include foods as diverse as bats, frogs, and road-killed turtles, Mississippi Kites are adaptable and opportunistic hunters, especially when compared with relatives such as the Everglade, or Snail, Kite with its specialized bill structure and restricted diet.

Unfortunately, until fieldwork covers more of their range, we can only assume that the food habits of Mississippi Kites remain similar throughout the year. The data summarized here are solely for the summer months in North America. No studies, however cursory, hint at the diet for Mississippi Kites during the many months they spend in passage to and wintering in Central and South America.

2

Feeding Behavior

The aerial skills of Mississippi Kites are well known to anyone who has spent even a few moments watching the birds course overhead on a lazy summer day. For the most part, these sleek, pointed-winged hawks sweep insects from the air. But other methods may be used, depending on the prey at hand.

Mississippi Kites typically hunt while leisurely circling over grasslands or other relatively open habitats with scattered brush or trees. Some glean their food above golf courses, campuses, and city parks. When hunting, kites normally glide on set wings at altitudes of no more than 300 feet. This altitude undoubtedly reflects the aerial patterns of insect movements, which in turn seem related to the columns of hot air (thermals) rising from the ground. Kites thus hunt at relatively low altitudes in the cool, steel-wool overcast of a southern morning, then gradually carve their circular glides at increasing heights as the day warms and thermals carry flying insects higher into the clearing sky.

When beetles or other airborne insects are sighted, Mississippi Kites fold their wings and plunge in what falconers call a "stoop"—a rocketlike descent ending with a curved, braking swoop as the birds close on their targets. As one observer in Alabama noted, Mississippi Kites stoop at shallow angles, usually of 20 degrees or less. Evidently stooping for prey as erratic in flight as insects is not a precise art, for we have noticed that kites often conclude a stoop with a compensating half roll or a few quick wing beats. At the end of a successful stoop, the bird quickly levels its flight path and resumes its slow flight, the hapless prey securely held in the grasp of strong talons.

The dean of wildlife biologists in Texas, A. S. Jackson, relates that plumes of smoke from grass fires send long-distance signals across the plains to hungry kites. Thus attracted, the birds hunt above and windward of the smoke, where they stoop at insects fleeing the flames.

Mississippi Kites also seize cicadas and other insects scared into flight by grazing animals, including livestock. This manner of feeding somewhat resembles the well-known association between livestock and cattle egrets, although the egrets snatch their prey with jabs from their pointed bills as they walk beside their accommodating allies, whereas the kites snag insects disturbed into flight. The observant Jackson tells of an incident on the sandhills of Hemphill County, Texas, hard by the rolling breaks of the Canadian River. After scaring up three deer, which quickly bounded out of sight, he nonetheless was able to track their movements for some time afterward because of the kites that followed from above, stooping to the cicadas flushed before the retreating deer.

Kites also employ a second method of hunting in which they sweep prey directly from tall grasses and the upper branches of shrubs and trees. We have not seen this behavior, but if it actually follows the intense, if anthropomorphic, account of Audubon, it must be a spectacular sight to behold. In *Birds of America*, he writes:

> [The kite] glances towards the earth with his fiery eye; sweeps along, now with the gentle breeze, now against it; seizes here and there the high-flying giddy bug, and allays his hunger without fatigue to wing or talon. Suddenly, he spies some creeping thing, that changes, like the chameleon from vivid green to dull brown, to escape his notice. It is the red-throated panting lizard [Carolina anole] that has made its way to the highest branch of a tree in quest of food. Casting upwards a

Green anoles, according to John James Audubon, were among the foods of Mississippi Kites. These fleet-footed lizards are also known as Carolina anoles, but Audubon called them "red-throated panting lizards" because of the pinkish dewlap displayed by males. The range of the species largely coincides with the distribution of Mississippi Kites in the southeastern United States. Photo courtesy of Jack Dermid.

sidelong look of fear, it remains motionless, so well does it know the prowess of the bird of prey; but its caution is vain; it has been perceived, its fate is sealed, and the next moment it is swept away.

At times Mississippi Kites hunt from a perch from which they locate and attack prey, behavior known as "hawking." Fitch watched kites hunt in this manner for insects (probably dragonflies) over a pool in Kansas. The birds made short flights from a tree where 16 were perched, seized their prey, and then returned to their perches. In another setting, the kites

Still-standing dead trees—known as "snags"—provide important wild-life habitat, including perches from which hawks can search for prey. Skeletonlike trunks of dead trees are the most common form of snags, but Mississippi Kites prefer perches on the dead branches of living trees. Photo courtesy of Richard L. Glinski.

hawked from the tops of fence posts, skimming grasshoppers in low passes over a pasture. In the latter instance, the low-flying glides of the birds may have flushed the insects, which then were "picked off" as they rushed to escape. Hawking behavior occurs more commonly in the early morning and late afternoon, times when thermals and other winds are not available to assist with soaring.

Hawking from "snags"—dead trees—within 500 feet of nests accounted for 41 percent of the food—mostly cicadas—kites in Arizona brought to their nestlings. Snags have other ecological values for wildlife—among them, foraging sites for woodpeckers—but snags are typically embodied as the skeletal remains of dead trees still standing in place. For Mississippi Kites, however, dead limbs in a canopy of otherwise living trees are favored as hunting perches. Thus, in Arizona, the presence of tall cottonwoods, replete with snags of dead limbs, protruding above an understory of saltcedar offers optimal foraging habitat for Mississippi Kites. Cicadas thrive in the saltcedar, and the cottonwoods provide perches from which the kites can hawk. Unfortunately, riparian environments where these species interact in their own microcosm often suffer from human abuses, no doubt with predictable results for Mississippi Kite populations.

Finally, Mississippi Kites at times secure food after alighting on the ground, although this behavior is not a common hunting strategy for this or any other species of raptor. Otherwise, it is difficult to explain the presence of road kills, ground beetles (which, as implied, don't fly), and certain other foods that occasionally turn up in the diet of Mississippi Kites. James W. Parker, who spent several years closely observing kites, has seen large numbers of kites alight along a stream where they bathed, drank, and possibly hunted for frogs in the shallow water. We also have seen kites hopping and cavorting along the grassy banks of a spring-fed rivulet in a canyon on the High Plains, but we cannot say for certain that hunting was part of these activities.

Unlike most raptors, which perch atop an outcrop or snag when devouring their foods, Mississippi Kites generally feed on the wing—an aerial feat of no mean consequence. We watched this behavior on a fine June morning in Texas when, from our own perch just below the rugged edge of the Caprock in Yellow House Canyon, we were in perfect position to observe a yearling kite feeding on a choice morsel no more than a few dozen yards overhead. This bird, having moments before secured a large-bodied insect on the plains just beyond the rimrock, adroitly tilted its head downward while extending forward the leg bearing its prey, then carefully tore away and devoured bits of its prize, all the while floating effortlessly toward the canyon. In just a few moments of languid gliding on set wings, the kite had consumed its victim with two or three well-placed bites. Unsatiated, the kite resumed its searches unaware—or perhaps uncaring—of the enraptured humans below. For us this was a singular event, but in reality this was a routine meal among eons of similar feedings. And the few words hastily scribbled in our field journals scarcely reflected our long-standing admiration for the considerable skills with which evolution has endowed predators.

Kites may be more delicate gourmands than our description implies. A. C. Bent notes that Mississippi Kites carefully trim unwanted parts from certain kinds of prey. The wings and legs of grasshoppers, for example, are pruned from the insect's body, and only the abdomens of cicadas are consumed. The rest is simply dropped. The under plumage of Mississippi Kites often may be somewhat discolored and slightly sticky, which puzzled one ornithologist until he realized that this area is the bird's dining table while feeding in flight. Exudate from partially devoured insects gradually soils the feathers in this area, perhaps also contributing to the sweetish odor one detects when holding a kite.

3
Drinking

Little is known about the drinking behavior of many birds, although there are such remarkable examples as Sand Grouse, which in some of the most arid spots on earth daily transport water many miles in their breast plumage to thirsty chicks. We have seen Mississippi Kites drinking at a small creek in Texas— or at least that seemed to be what they were doing—but our observations took place at a distance, and our binoculars revealed few details. Other observers have noted kites in shallow water, drinking and, at times, seeking frogs.

4
Sexual Size Dimorphism and Diet

For most vertebrates, individuals of one sex often differ in appearance from the other, a condition known as sexual dimorphism (e.g., colorful males and drab females, of which Cardinals and Mallards offer prominent examples). Body size also may differ between the sexes. Males typically have larger bodies than females, and for birds, this difference is usually the case regardless of whether there is dimorphism in plumage. Curiously, however, the reverse is often the case in a few groups of birds, including hawks: the females are larger, often markedly so, than males in many (although not all) birds in the falconiform group. Larger-sized females also occur in another major group of raptors, the owls.

The enigma of larger females in these groups of birds has prompted long-standing debate, often including the role that food habits might play in this form of dimorphism. But first of all, are female Mississippi Kites larger than males, and if so, by how much? For scale, we will highlight the research of ornithologists Noel Snyder and James Wiley and compare the Mississippi Kite with the Sharp-shinned Hawk, an accipiter found in open woodlands across North America (see Table 2).

Table 2

	Wing (Chord)		Bill		Weight		
	M	F	M	F	M	F	Index
Mississippi Kite	294	300	15.8	16.2	248	314	4.2
Sharp-shinned Hawk	170	203	9.9	12.7	102	179	20.4

Note: Wing and bill measurements are in millimeters, and weights are in grams. The index combines the three measurements for an overall comparison between species (see Appendix B). An index of 1.0 indicates no difference in wing size, bill length, or weight between males and females.

A comparison of the indexes in the last column shows a relatively slight difference between male and female Mississippi Kites, whereas the magnitude of difference between male and female Sharp-shinned Hawks is about five times greater. That is, female Mississippi Kites are only slightly larger than their male counterparts, but female Sharp-shinned Hawks are much larger than male "sharpies." In fact, Sharp-shinned Hawks show the greatest degree of sexual size dimorphism of all North American hawks. Females not only are far larger structurally, but weigh nearly twice as much as males.

Diet is another way in which these species differ. Mississippi Kites, as we have seen, feed largely on insects. In contrast, the diet of Sharp-shinned Hawks consists almost entirely of small birds. Indeed, a strong correlation exists between the features of diet and dimorphism, as was confirmed when Snyder and Wiley compared a larger sample of species in the same way, as follows. In addition to Sharp-shinned Hawks, Peregrine Falcons (index of 15.7), Cooper's Hawks (14.8), and other bird-eating species show considerable size dimorphism when compared to Ospreys (5.1), American Kestrels (4.6), Red-tailed Hawks (7.8), and others that prey on fishes, invertebrates, or small mammals.

The indexes for other kites regularly occurring in parts of the United States, which never or only infrequently feed on birds, agree with this line of evidence. Everglade Kite (0.8; snails), Swallow-tailed Kite (1.1; insects), and Black-shouldered Kite (1.4; mice) all show only slight sexual dimorphism in size. The index for Mississippi Kites (4.2), while clearly aligned with the group that does not eat birds, inexplicably is the highest among the kites studied by Snyder and Wiley.

Among the theories concerning size dimorphism in hawks is the notion that it enables the birds to utilize a wider spectrum of food resources. The larger females seek larger prey while the males hunt for smaller foods, or so the theory states. But to the extent this may be true, it scarcely explains why the female and not the male is the larger of the two sexes. The same array of foods could just as easily be secured by large males and small females, with evolution following the more usual pathway of larger males and smaller females. Yet this has not happened, and the enigma remains.

In the case of Mississippi Kites, the potential menu of insect foods does not vary greatly in size, and the evolutionary pressure for dimorphism may act in reverse. Such prey as ants or gnats are so small as to provide little return for the effort, thus compelling kites to seek insects of a more rewarding size. Within this group, however, grasshoppers, cicadas, crickets, and most beetles concurrently represent both the upper and lower size limits. In other words, the insect-dominated menu of kites lacks the range in sizes that would occur if reptiles, birds, or mammals were the principal foods. Thus, with such a limited range (in terms of body size) in the pool of suitable insect prey, male and female kites necessarily select the same foods, and dimorphism in these birds is limited in comparison with other species of hawks.

Yet another hypothesis concerns a division of labor. Because the females in many species of hawks remain at the nest in charge of the young, the smaller males do the hunting and therefore bring food better suited for the nestlings. Again, the idea that the food is smaller *because* the males are smaller is a notion that seems to fail the test of logic, confusing effect with cause. Moreover, females are fully capable of tearing large prey into morsels of a size their young could swallow.

There are other theories as to why female hawks are larger than males, but none has been proved beyond reasonable doubt. At this point, it seems enough to observe that many mysteries, among them sexual size dimorphism, remain in nature. Such is the stuff of biology.

Conservation and Management

I
Kites in Cities

We have thus far focused on Mississippi Kites in more-or-less rural settings, many of which are not greatly different now than when our young nation was still exploring its frontiers. Today, kites still float on thermals rising over the prairies— grasslands grazed by docile cattle rather than wild bison, true, but still grasslands. Kites also still seek riparian woodlands, re-grettably one of nature's more plundered environments, but nonetheless fortunately still intact in many places.

But there is another environment, entirely human in origin, that today attracts numbers of Mississippi Kites: the city and its own peculiar milieu. Normally, we associate exotic species— Starlings, Pigeons, and House Sparrows—with urban settings. At first blush, anyone watching the graceful hunting of a Mis-sissippi Kite above a cottonwood gallery might not transpose such a sight to a residential area, a busy college campus, a park or courthouse lawn, or a manicured golf course. Yet, in New Mexico, a colony of some 40 kites breeding at a municipal park and golf course is the largest in the state.

Most urban populations of Mississippi Kites occur, at least for now, west of the Mississippi River, ignoring essentially identical urban habitat throughout the forested regions in the southeastern United States. Interestingly, the urban popula-tion nesting in Garden City, Kansas, in the opinion of one biologist, may have been the source of those kites that have moved upstream along the Arkansas River into Colorado.

Not many species of raptors adapt to city life, but among the few is the Peregrine Falcon. Peregrines were among the species whose eggshells were perilously thinned by pesticide accumu-lations and thus became—and remain—an endangered spe-cies. In cities, these magnificent hunters nest on window ledges of skyscrapers high above traffic-clogged streets. The window ledges, usually at heights of 25 or more stories, are the urban analogs of the sheer cliff faces where peregrines have traditionally nested through millennia of wilderness life. Then, too, in the city the often obnoxious populations of pigeons offer a ready supply of prey for these swiftest of all birds. Cities thus became a vital component in the rebuilding of peregrine populations in North America.

For Mississippi Kites, however, the tenor of city life may not always be quite so sanguine as it is for Peregrine Falcons. Although kites successfully nest in trees along busy thoroughfares in such large cities as Lubbock, Texas (population 190,000), they also choose golf courses and parks as nesting habitat. And it is often in such places that problems arise. Here the birds may react vigorously to passersby on the lawns and fairways below nest trees, especially during the latter stages of the nesting cycle. The aerial dive-bombing, according to expert James W. Parker, usually ends when the young birds fledge from their nests.

Golfers are most often subject to attacks, but mail carriers, too, may have more than troublesome dogs to complain about in those neighborhoods where kites nest. One woman, walking through a housing development in an Oklahoma woodland, lost her hair net to an irate kite, but the attack fortunately caused no other harm. Such aerial bombardments, while undoubtedly frightening, seldom produce injuries. Still, even the odd scalp laceration is understandably more than enough to upset the immediate victim—and to inspire some mention in the local newspaper.

A study of more than 900 such attacks at a golf course in New Mexico indicated that kites actually struck humans in only 3 percent of the dives. Furthermore, the strikes were limited to just two of the 11 pairs of birds nesting at the golf course, and of these, all but one of the attacks were initiated by a single pair of particularly aggressive kites.

We suspect that, on occasion, and despite stringent laws against such things, the operators of golf courses may terminate troublesome kites "with extreme prejudice." Nests containing eggs or chicks might be destroyed in anticipation that the loss might disperse the adult birds to more hospitable locations, or perhaps a pellet gun might silently rid the fairways of the offending birds once and for all. Indeed, residents of a Kansas town at one time did overreact to the diving behavior of nesting kites, with the result that 28 birds were summarily shot. While deplorable, such actions nonetheless provided the stimulus for more enlightened management. Based on their respective studies of such situations, biologists James W. Parker and Antonio L. Gennaro recommend several measures, which we condense here:

1. Deployment of street signs and posters at sites where the attacks occur.
2. Public education using popular articles while downplaying the sensational aspects of the attacks.
3. Discouraging the reuse of nesting sites with dummy kites and nests.
4. As a final resort, removing and transplanting eggs and chicks to the nests of kites breeding in rural environments.

The adaptability of Mississippi Kites also may serve as a means for educating the public about predators and predation, a suggestion posed by biologists in New Mexico. Unlike most predators, kites are not secretive, and numbers of the birds can be readily viewed capturing their prey. Hence, with public observation areas strategically located in and near cities, Mississippi Kites can serve as a highly popular attraction and an educational tool that focuses on one of the more poorly understood components of nature.

Elsewhere in the world, Black Kites—perhaps the world's most abundant species of kite—also thrive in cities. Thousands of Black Kites breed in the trees bordering crowded city streets throughout their huge geographical range in Asia, Africa, and Australia, an adaptation that noted authority Leslie Brown believes has increased their numbers. In their urban environments, however, Black Kites are far less fastidious than Mississippi Kites, whose summer diet remains essentially no different between urban and rural settings. In cities, Black Kites glean refuse from the streets and, remarkably, often snatch food directly from tabletops and open stalls in busy markets. In the past, we have observed the bold feeding behavior of Black Kites in the populous venue of Dakar, Senegal, where the birds are more common than pigeons. Hundreds sail just over the rooftops of buildings whose ironwork façades recall a bygone era of French colonialism in western Africa. Nonetheless, as extraordinary as these relationships may be, we hope—for aesthetic reasons—that Mississippi Kites never realize the same degree of urbanization as Black Kites. For us, Mississippi Kites symbolize not the dusty streets of a southwestern city, but the open plains and riparian woodlands of an unspoiled landscape.

2
Predators and People

Human regard for predators is rife with prejudice, fear, and ecological error. We have fueled these misjudgments with the long-standing conviction that predators were competitors, and sometimes with the tenuous view of ourselves as hapless prey. Wolves, in particular, have suffered because of myth and legend. Bedtime stories taint the minds of toddlers with tales of wolf attacks. Predators are, of course, normal components of a healthy environment, and it is not off the mark to view their absence as an indication of an imbalanced ecological community. Henry David Thoreau, the village crank of Concord and natural philosopher for the rest of us, likened a diminished fauna to a "tribe of Indians that had lost all its warriors."

Thankfully, that barbaric relic, the bounty system, has largely been eliminated from public policy, but not before wolves were completely erased from most of the United States. At least one western state still regards mountain lions as varmints that may be freely eliminated at any time and by any means, and plans for the reintroduction of gray wolves face stiff opposition as we near the end of the twentieth century. Still, much of society has matured in an ecological sense. The vital role of wolves and mountain lions now is understood and appreciated by a large segment of the American public—and the intrinsic right of predators to exist as free fellow creatures of the planet is fiercely defended by many environmentalists.

Hawks and other raptors have not been immune from the hatred and persecution directed toward predators, at times even by naturalists who ought to have known better. None other than Alexander Wilson, on finding the tattered victim of an unspecified hawk, was unable to suppress the harshness of a death sentence:

> . . . passing along the edge of the rocks, I found fragments of the wings and broken feathers of a wood thrush killed by the hawk, which I contemplated with unfeigned regret, and not without a determination to retaliate on the first of these murderers I could meet with.

Although the sinister tone of revenge for the thrush's violent death is certainly clear, there is no record that Wilson ever gunned down hawks other than those he wanted as models for his now famous paintings.

Among the earliest attempts at what was then considered "game" management was a bounty system that often included hawks—and the generic and ill-founded designation "chicken hawk" for just about any bird of prey certainly didn't help matters. In 1885, Pennsylvania enacted a hawk-and-owl bounty law—known at the time as the "scalp act"—which provided for a payment of 50 cents per raptor scalp. Within two years, 180,000 hawk and owl scalps were bountied, for which the taxpayers of Pennsylvania parted with $90,000—big money for the day. Yet one estimate of the program indicated that farmers saved just about $1 for each $1,205 paid out in bounties! But the folly of the bounty on raptors was not limited to direct payments. Fields and orchards soon were overrun with mice and other vermin to the point that farmers requested repeal of the bounty law, which happened two years later, but not before crop damage had added another $2 million to the program's cost. Even so, the idiocy of bounties continued in other areas well into the current century. Maryland paid bounties on nearly 90,000 hawks between 1925 and 1930, and Alaska's territorial government authorized a $2 bounty on Bald Eagles in 1917. By 1952, when the bounty ended in Alaska, more than 128,000 Bald Eagles had been cashiered.

Just before the beginning of World War I, William T. Hornaday, a well-known conservationist and director of the New York Zoo, rallied public concern for the nation's dwindling wildlife populations. In *Our Vanishing Wild Life*, Hornaday wrote that "beyond question, it is both desirable and necessary" that predators of what he considered desirable (read "huntable") birds should be eliminated. Thus, quail and grouse had value and raptors did not, at least in Hornaday's view. He singled out two species of accipiters and two falcons for an immediate "sentence of death." To be fair to Hornaday and his time, he did not overlook other threats to wildlife—including Italian immigrants and poor Southerners! Perhaps we shouldn't be too hard on Dr. Hornaday. He gained much-needed protection for the few bison still remaining at the end of the last century, which remains a far more positive contribution to wildlife conservation than his ill-conceived policies toward predators.

During this era, wildlife biologists began toiling with a variety of field studies designed to unlock the riddles of predation. Analyses of the stomach contents or droppings of predatory animals were one approach, but the results could be misleading and certainly did not reveal *how* predators secured their food. Predators might scavenge already dead animals as well as make outright kills, but neither situation would be clearly indicated from the contents still identifiable in an acidic stomach or a weathered dropping. Also, such contents scarcely told whether the victim was indeed healthy when killed or, as may be commonplace, if the prey was already weakened by starvation, disease, or injury and therefore predisposed to a predator's attack.

Industrious field research also determined that predators

were seldom as efficient as one might believe from folklore and woodsmen's tales. In fact, most predators expend a great deal of time and energy for the amount of food actually secured. Simply put, most predators stay hungry most of the time. Even the legendary hunting abilities of wolves seem grossly exaggerated. One particularly thorough study on Isle Royale revealed that of 77 moose "tested" by wolves, only six were killed—a success rate of about 8 percent. And the chase for food is little better for raptors. In Europe, careful study of the hunting behavior of predatory birds, which included falcons, hawks, and eagles, determined that only 7.6 percent of more than 680 attacks actually yielded any food for the effort. The success rate varied by species from 4.5 to 10.8 percent, but the message from this and similar research is clear: raptors and other predators rarely live up to their reputations as efficient killers.

Meanwhile, bird-watching was one of the nonconsumptive outdoor activities that flowered in response to the changing twentieth-century environmental vision. This cadre of largely self-taught naturalists—they refer to themselves as "birders" who go "birding"—became, and remains, an effective force in the never-ending political battles on behalf of wildlife. Birders also joined forces with the Sierra Club and other mainstream environmental organizations as well as the more radical groups such as Earth First! Among their concerns is the protection of raptors, for instance the Northern Spotted Owl in old-growth forests of the Pacific Northwest and the Northern Goshawk populations nesting in threatened forests of the Southwest.

The changing attitude toward raptors is perhaps best illustrated at Hawk Mountain, Pennsylvania, where the craggy features of the landscape funnel large numbers of migrating hawks southward every fall. In past decades, the availability of the hawks soaring at more-or-less eye-level on the mountain's overlooks was ready made for those who believed their shotguns could provide a valuable service for improving nature. In keeping with Dr. Hornaday's teachings, fewer hawks meant more game. Besides, this was a way to sharpen one's eye for the hunting season. The resulting slaughter seems unimaginable

[83]

given today's sensitivities, but each autumn thousands of hawks nonetheless were felled as convenient live targets. Today, the grim tally is recalled in the yellowing photographs of proud gunners and their ill-gotten plunder.

In 1932, Richard Pough, trained as an industrial engineer and soon to become a noted ornithologist and conservationist, discovered the carnage at Hawk Mountain and alerted Rosalie Edge, a member of what was known as the Emergency Conservation Committee. She immediately became an indefatigable champion for the protection of both the migrating hawks and the unique mountainside in Pennsylvania. The outcome was the formation of the Hawk Mountain Sanctuary Association, a privately funded organization that today enjoys the support of some 8,000 members. Each year more than 50,000 visitors travel to the sanctuary in response to this notable effort at wildlife conservation and, of course, to witness the majesty of hawk migrations no longer punctuated by the sounds of gunshots.

Similarly, Witmer Stone described the annual kill of hawks moving southward through Cape May at the tip of New Jersey. At its worst, the slaughter claimed as many as 1,400 hawks in a single day in 1920. Daily "bags" of 50 or 60 hawks per gunner were commonplace, with the ill-fated birds hauled off in peach baskets. Why carry home baskets of dead hawks? To eat! One estimate suggests that fully 95 percent of the gunners used the hawks for food. Although understandably embarrassed by the event, famed artist-ornithologist Roger Tory Peterson in 1935 dined on a meal of 20 Sharp-shinned Hawks, "broiled like squabs," in the home of a Cape May hunter. As for taste, he found his main course "good." By 1964, when Peterson penned his confession, hawk-shooting was over at Cape May, and state law protected all birds of prey in New Jersey. And we doubt that Mr. Peterson ever again feasted on a meal of hawks.

From the 1920s onward, the tide slowly turned as sensitivities toward nature steadily matured. New ecological knowledge spread into the consciousness of American life when writers such as Aldo Leopold and Rachel Carson promoted a less

Hawks of several species once were shot at Hawk Mountain, Pennsylvania, a senseless slaughter that eventually led to the area becoming a celebrated preserve for migrating raptors. Shown here is a part of one day's kill in the early 1930s; this and similar photos were instrumental in publicizing the carnage. Large numbers of hawks also were shot each autumn at Cape May, New Jersey. Photo courtesy of Hawk Mountain Sanctuary Association.

human-centered and more biocentric vision of environmental ethics. Leopold, the premier philosopher-scientist of wildlife conservation, had himself experienced a transformation in his regard for predators—a turnabout poignantly described in his essay *Thinking Like a Mountain*. Outdoor and nature writers for popular magazines educated the public with new ideas about the integrity of biological communities, including the presence of predators. In this climate, bounty systems faded into well-deserved oblivion, and state conservation agencies gradually turned from a narrow focus on game management to the greater concern for wildlife of all kinds.

For the management of migratory birds, the Migratory Bird Treaty and its implementation in the United States via the Migratory Bird Treaty Act were godsends long-awaited by conservationists. These landmarks were signed in 1916 and 1918, respectively, and marked the end of two incredibly exploitative practices: spring waterfowl hunting and shooting herons and egrets for their plumes. Migrant songbirds—those that ate insects were given special mention in the treaty—were granted full protection, as were Whooping Cranes and selected other species of birds that migrated between Canada and the United States. A similar treaty with Mexico was concluded in 1936. Yet, in keeping with the prevailing sentiment of the era, hawks were not mentioned in these acts, and insofar as federal law was concerned, birds of prey remained subject to uncontrolled killing by any means at any time. Moreover, this omission denied protection to our national emblem, and not until 1940 did Congress enact the Bald Eagle Protection Act, later expanded to include Golden Eagles. Hence, unless raptors were protected by the laws of individual states, as some were, an open season on hawks and owls was in effect well into the present century. Finally, in 1972, when the treaty with Mexico was amended, hawks and allied species were granted the full weight of federal protection from indiscriminate killing such as had occurred at Hawk Mountain and Cape May.

Raptors eventually were included in the management of public lands when the Snake River Birds of Prey Area was established in 1980 by executive action of Cecil D. Andrus, Secretary of the Interior (a smaller area of public land at the same site was protected in 1971 by Secretary Rogers C. B. Morton). Managed by the Bureau of Land Management, the site includes about 494,000 acres of rugged wilderness in southwestern Idaho, where more than 500 pairs of 15 species of raptors nest each year and another nine species regularly visit as migrants or winter residents. According to the bureau's management plan, the area was established "to protect and maintain the ecosystem necessary to support and perpetuate the densest and most diverse populations of eagles, hawks, falcons, owls, and other birds of prey ever recorded."

With the mounting public appreciation and admiration for hawks and other raptors, professional biologists likewise increased their attention to birds of prey. As one response, nesting platforms designed for Ospreys, a species devastated by pesticides, were erected throughout much of the species' breeding range in North America. As another, the *Journal of Raptor Research*, founded in 1967, is today a major publication in the abundant scientific literature about birds.

Mississippi Kites are not without their own history of persecution. In depression-era Oklahoma, famed ornithologist George M. Sutton expressed great concern for the fate of Mississippi Kites, not because of shooting, but because of overzealous egg collecting. Because collectors prized the eggs of Mississippi Kites—in the parlance of the trade, these were "good" eggs—purveyors of bird eggs often stockpiled large supplies of kite eggs for sale to amateur oologists. Kites breeding in Oklahoma were especially vulnerable to this form of exploitation because their nests were accessible in low-growing shrubs. As Sutton noted, with no more than a step ladder and a few dimes for farm boys, a collector from the East could accumulate large numbers of kite eggs in short order. Inevitably, as the nesting population dwindled, fancy prices accrued for the stockpile of eggs awaiting sale. Contemplating the situation, Sutton despaired of a springtime in the shinnery country of Oklahoma with "no kite at play among the clouds."

Beginning with Peter Custis, scientists have collected kites as a means of studying natural history. Skin collections clearly document the presence of kites in specific locales; a specimen in hand also offers close examination of birds whose identification otherwise might be difficult or impossible to determine. Even so, the somewhat maudlin reports in the older scientific literature can be unsettling. As a sample, consider the words of Albert Franklyn Ganier. Based on his report, published in 1902, Ganier watched two kites feeding their almost-fledged young at a nest in Mississippi. After watching the nest for an hour or two for several days, Ganier wrote, "[my] affection for [the young bird] grew so strong that my gun was commissioned to add his skin to my collection." A few days later, Ganier carried axe and gun to another nest in a cottonwood some 40 inches in diameter: "[although the] task seemed a big one . . . I had the satisfaction of seeing the big fellow come crashing to the ground [with the prospect of adding] two more immature specimens for my collection." Ganier was disappointed: the nest was empty. Ever the scientist, with his axe-handle technique Ganier was able to determine that the cottonwood was 131 feet tall and that the kite nest was a lofty 119 feet above ground.

Then, too, Mississippi Kites were shot merely because they were birds of prey. Much of this probably was idle plinking at accessible—and remarkably tame—live targets. But not always, as Sutton mentions that a zealous game warden might shoot 200–300 kites, no doubt in the mistaken belief that next fall a few more coveys of quail would stir on the windy plains.

3
Winter Problems

At least two circumstances threaten migrant birds wintering in the Southern Hemisphere, including the Mississippi Kite as well as a host of warblers and other songbirds. The first is the unchecked deforestation now laying bare vast tracts of irre-

placeable rain forest and other tropical woodlands in much of
Central and South America. Alarmed by the destruction, ornithologists and environmentalists suggest that this loss of
habitat contributes to the declining populations of several species of songbirds, all of which winter in tropical forests. We
need not repeat here how deforestation produces short-term
economic gains and long-term ecological liabilities, but we can
speculate that it might be only a matter of time before Mississippi Kites, too, respond to the loss of winter habitat. Clearly,
the apparent security of Mississippi Kites for a few short
months during the breeding season ought not lull our concerns
for the birds' safe future.

A second concern involves pesticides. Thanks to the seminal
work of Rachel Carson, DDT and other organochlorines that
biomagnify are now banned in the United States. Yet American chemical companies still produce and export immense ton-
nages of these compounds to Third World nations, including
those where Mississippi Kites overwinter. Moreover, few, if
any, regulations govern the application of pesticides elsewhere
in the Americas. Hence, kites and other birds might still accumulate harmful amounts of poison during the several months
they spend in other countries. Fortunately, the short food
chain of Mississippi Kites apparently thwarted eggshell thinning when organochlorines were still used legally in the United
States. Unfortunately, virtually nothing is known about the
food habits of kites during the winter months, and similar protection is not assured.

These two issues are not unrelated. As farmland is cleared
from the forests in Central and South America, kites may be
forced into a diet dominated by insects associated with agriculture. And if the crops on the newly cleared lands are heavily
treated with pesticides, as seems likely, then Mississippi Kites
may experience much greater exposure to harmful chemicals
than before. In any case, until more is learned about the winter
ecology of Mississippi Kites, no plan for their conservation and
management can be truly comprehensive.

4
Protected Areas

Mississippi Kites are not immediately threatened across the broad range of their distribution in the United States. Still, because of the few kites occurring within its borders, New Mexico has placed the kite on its list of endangered species. In this and similar locations, small populations may be disrupted easily, and ecological change—especially in the kite's range along High Plains and Southwest desert rivers—could alter the situation quickly. One change concerns the maturity and subsequent decay of trees in the thousands of linear miles of shelterbelts that once helped draw Mississippi Kites westward in the 1930s. Other shelterbelts were cut down in the 1970s, when farm policies encouraged fence-to-fence planting. Much of that land has now been reclaimed in grass by the Conservation Reserve Program (CRP), but the shelterbelt habitat for kites is already gone. The CRP is encouraging planting of new shelterbelts, but the scale will probably never equal the 218 million trees planted during the 1930s.

At a pace only slightly slower than in the tropical rain forests, riparian habitat is fast disappearing in the kite's southeastern range, where Custis, Wilson, and Audubon first brought the Mississippi Kite to the attention of the world. Much of the modern world apparently values soybeans more than cypress swamps and Mississippi Kites. Along Arizona's Gila and Salt rivers, and in many other saltcedar–infested floodplains across the Southwest, the Army Corps of Engineers busily clears brush, thereby destroying cicada habitat and threatening several highly localized populations of kites. Additionally, we should note the importance of riparian habitat as pathways of dispersal. On the plains of Kansas, for example, riparian habitat along the Arkansas and Cimmarron rivers apparently acted as travel lanes for kites moving westward into Colorado.

Nor are Mississippi Kites always regarded warmly in those urban centers where they have become common summer visitors. Here kites are sometimes considered no-account "trash birds" that harass golfers and dive-bomb sidewalk strollers, and on rare occasions cause scalp lacerations and even bicycle-auto collisions.

Because kite colonies tend to be widely scattered, not every municipal or state park, or national grassland, or Bureau of Land Management tract across the southern United States acts to preserve Mississippi Kites. It is possible that one day environmentalists will want to set aside small preserves specifically to protect nesting kites. Meanwhile, Mississippi Kites are among the many species that would benefit from the kinds of public land acquisitions proposed for the Great Plains. Recent and upcoming acquisitions by the Nature Conservancy in places such as western Oklahoma and western Texas surely will be a boon for kites. So would a tallgrass prairie national park in either Oklahoma or Kansas. And the viability of the Mississippi Kite as a wild species would virtually be guaranteed if the federal government ever establishes a wilderness park in the canyonlands along the Llano Estacado Escarpment in western Texas.

The Southern High Plains may be one region in the United States where the prophets of environmental doom will find themselves vindicated. The unrelenting drawdown of the Ogallala Aquifer—which underwrites an irrigated economy across a huge region—together with the constant threat of more dust bowls and of global warming, targets the Southern Plains as a likely region for ecological difficulties in the twenty-first century.

But if Rutgers University scholars Frank and Deborah Popper's controversial vision of a "Buffalo Commons" of public lands ever comes true for the great American interior, then it will likely come first to the Southern Plains. If so, along with bison, pronghorns, mountain lions, and perhaps even wolves, as they regain their former place in the ancient wilderness order, Mississippi Kites will be among the beneficiaries.

For that matter, so will we.

Common and Scientific Names of Plants and Animals Mentioned in the Text

Plants

Nomenclature for plants follows F. W. Gould (1969), Texas Plants; a Checklist and Ecological Summary, rev. ed. Texas Agricultural and Experiment Station, Texas A&M University, College Station.

Shortleaf pine	*Pinus echinata*
Loblolly pine	*Pinus taeda*
Baldcypress	*Taxodium distichum*
Spanishmoss	*Tillandsia usneoides*
Cottonwood	*Populus* spp.
Black willow	*Salix nigra*
Pecan	*Juglans illinoensis*
Black walnut	*Juglans nigra*
White oak	*Quercus alba*
Red oak	*Quercus falcata*
Shinnery oak	*Quercus havardii*
Blackjack oak	*Quercus marilandica*
Live oak	*Quercus virginiana*
Hackberry	*Celtis laevigata*
American elm	*Ulmus americana*
Siberian elm	*Ulmus pumila*
Osage orange	*Maclura pomifera*
Magnolia	*Magnolia* spp.
Sweetgum	*Liquidambar styraciflua*
Mesquite	*Prosopis glandulosa*
Locust	*Robinia* spp.
Sumac	*Rhus* spp.
Soapberry	*Sapindus drummondi*
Saltcedar [Tamarisk]	*Tamarix gallica*
Tupelo	*Nyssa* spp.
Persimmon	*Diospyros virginiana*

Invertebrates

Nomenclature for insects follows D. J. Borror and R. E. White (1970), A Field Guide to the Insects. Houghton Mifflin, Boston. Various sources were consulted for other species.

Apple snail	*Pomacea* spp. (e.g., *P. paludosa*)
Dragonflies	Aeshnidae and Libellulidae
Grasshoppers	Acrididae
Cave [camel] crickets	Gryllacrididae
Crickets	Gryllidae
Stink bugs	Pentatomidae
Cicadas	Cicadidae
Tiger beetles	Cicindelidae
Ground beetles	Carabidae
Wood-boring beetles	Buprestidae
Scarab [dung] beetles	Scarabaeidae
Weevils [likely snout beetles]	Curculionidae
Moths	Lepidoptera
Flies and gnats	Diptera
Ants	Formicidae
Wasps	Vespidae

Amphibians and Reptiles

Nomenclature for amphibians and reptiles follows R. Conant (1958), A Field Guide to Reptiles and Amphibians. Houghton Mifflin, Boston.

Bullfrog	*Rana catesbeiana*
Leopard frog	*Rana pipiens*
Ornate box turtle	*Terrapene ornata*
Carolina [green] anole	*Anolis carolinensis*
Horned lizards	*Phrynosoma* spp.
Rat snakes	*Elaphe* spp.

Birds

Nomenclature for North American birds follows American Ornithologists' Union (1983), Check-list of North American Birds, 6th ed. American Ornithologists' Union, Washington, D.C. Various sources were consulted for other species.

Secretarybird	*Sagittarius serpentarius*
White Stork	*Ciconia ciconia*
Mallard	*Anas platyrhynchos*
Osprey	*Pandion haliaetus*
Hook-billed Kite	*Chondrohierax uncinatus*
American Swallow-tailed Kite	*Elanoides forficatus*
Black-shouldered Kite	*Elanus caeruleus*
Snail [Everglade] Kite	*Rostrhamus sociabilis*
Mississippi Kite	*Ictinia mississippiensis*
Plumbeous Kite	*Ictinia plumbea*
Black Kite	*Milvus migrans*
Bald Eagle	*Haliaeetus leucocephalus*
Sea Eagle	*Haliaeetus albicilla*
Sharp-shinned Hawk	*Accipiter striatus*
Cooper's Hawk	*Accipiter cooperi*
Northern Goshawk	*Accipiter gentilis*
Harris' Hawk	*Parabuteo unicinctus*
Broad-winged Hawk	*Buteo platypterus*
Swainson's Hawk	*Buteo swainsoni*
Red-tailed Hawk	*Buteo jamaicensis*
Rough-legged Hawk	*Buteo lagopus*
Golden Eagle	*Aquila chrysaetos*
American Kestrel	*Falco sparverius*
Merlin	*Falco columbarius*
Peregrine Falcon	*Falco peregrinus*
Prairie Falcon	*Falco mexicanus*
Grouse	Phasianidae (e.g., *Tympanuchus* spp.)
Ruffed Grouse	*Bonasa umbellus*
Quail	Phasianidae (e.g., *Callipepla* spp.)
Bobwhite	*Colinus virginianus*
Whooping Crane	*Grus americana*

Sand Grouse	*Pterocles exustus*
Rock Dove ["Pigeon"]	*Columba livia*
Mourning Dove	*Zenaida macroura*
Barn Owl	*Tyto alba*
Great Horned Owl	*Bubo virginianus*
Spotted Owl	*Strix occidentalis*
Chimney Swift	*Chaetura pelagica*
Woodpeckers	Picidae (e.g., *Picoides villosus*)
Cliff Swallow	*Hirundo pyrrhonota*
Blue Jay	*Cyanocitta cristata*
Black-billed Magpie	*Pica pica*
American Crow	*Corvus brachyrhynchos*
Chihuahuan Raven	*Corvus cryptoleucus*
Wood Thrush	*Hylocichla mustelina*
Northern Mockingbird	*Mimus polyglottos*
Brown Thrasher	*Toxostoma rufum*
Shrikes	Laniidae (e.g., *Lanius ludovicianus*)
European Starling	*Sturnus vulgaris*
Wood warblers	Emberizidae (e.g., *Dendroica* spp.)
Red-winged Blackbird	*Agelaius phoeniceus*
Northern Oriole	*Icterus galbula*
Northern Cardinal	*Cardinalis cardinalis*
House Sparrow	*Passer domesticus*

Mammals

Nomenclature for mammals follows J. K. Jones, Jr., R. S. Hoffmann, D. W. Rice, C. Jones, R. J. Baker, and M. D. Engstrom (1992), Revised Checklist of North American Mammals North of Mexico, 1991. Occasional Papers, The Museum, Texas Tech University, Lubbock.

Western pipistrelle	*Pipistrellus hesperus*
Cottontail ["Rabbit"]	*Sylvilagus* spp.
Ground squirrel	*Spermophilus* spp.
Prairie dog	*Cynomys* spp.
Fox squirrel	*Sciurus niger*
Kangaroo rat	*Dipodomys* spp.

Deer mouse	*Peromyscus maniculatus*
Coyote	*Canis latrans*
Gray wolf	*Canis lupus*
Grizzly bear	*Ursus arctos*
Raccoon	*Procyon lotor*
Mountain lion	*Felis concolor*
White-tailed deer	*Odocoileus virginianus*
Moose	*Alces alces*
Pronghorn	*Antilocapra americana*
Bison	*Bison bison*

APPENDIX B
The Dimorphism Index

To determine the degree of sexual size dimorphism, average measurements of selected physical features (e.g., bill length) for each sex are employed to determine a "dimorphism index" (DI) using the following formula:

$$DI = \frac{\text{Average for females} - \text{Average for males}}{(\text{Average for females} + \text{Average for males}) \div 2} \times 100$$

Thus, using wing lengths for female (300 millimeters) and male (294 millimeters) Mississippi kites, we find

$$DI = \frac{300 - 294}{(300 + 294) \div 2} \times 100 = \frac{6}{297} \times 100 = 2.02$$

In this example, the dimorphism index is 2.02, which, when averaged with other indexes for bill size and weight, yields an overall index of 4.2 for Mississippi Kites.

The formula was developed by Storer (1966) and used by Snyder and Wiley (1976) in their monographic study of size dimorphism in hawks and owls. See references.

APPENDIX C
A Decade of Sightings by State

Many thousands of amateur ornithologists regularly—and irregularly—take to the field in search of birds. Armed with field guides and binoculars, this hearty cadre of dedicated "birders" often sight unusual occurrences of birds in places well outside the species' usual geographical distribution. Fortunately, the more serious birders among them report their observations, known as extralimital records, to the regional editors of the fraternity's premier journal, *American Birds*. This journal, which of course also reports more typical sightings of birds as well as the unusual, is published six times a year by the National Audubon Society and represents a wealth of data useful for many purposes. In the course of our studies of Mississippi Kites, we reviewed back issues of *American Birds* for the last decade or so, gleaning entries about Mississippi Kites. A sampling of these appear here, most of which are excerpted with little or no editing. For each, we cite the volume, issue, page, and year. Our purpose is to illustrate the growing frequency with which Mississippi Kites are sighted in a variety of places and times, along with other observations of interest. We thank all who submitted their observations to *American Birds*.

Arizona

A kite at Nogales on 11 May was a local first; the species is rarely seen away from its limited breeding area in Arizona. AB 37(5):899, 1983. A pair of Mississippi Kites again reported in a pecan grove north of Tucson, 17 May. AB 40(3):507, 1986. Several extralimital records, including those near the confluence of the Salt and Gila rivers, 29 June, near Buckeye on 30 June, and another at Cibola National Wildlife Refuge, 6 June. AB 40(5):1237, 1986. A Mississippi Kite at St. Johns, north of the White Mountains, 16 June, provided the first record north of the Mogollon Rim by many miles. AB 41(5):1471, 1987.

Arkansas

During 2–3 July, 65 Mississippi Kites counted in Desha County; as mysteriously as they came, they disappeared. AB 39(5):922, 1985.

California

Record of a Mississippi Kite for Death Valley, 28–29 May, the sixth for the area; also a kite on 30 May in Inyo County, the first for the Owens Valley. AB 36(5):893, 1982. A kite at Long Beach, 21 June, and another near Imperial Beach on 18 July are the third and fouth records for the coast. AB 36(6):1016, 1982. The species appears to be on the increase as a vagrant to California. AB 37(5):912, 1983. A rare, northern sighting was recorded in Tulare County, 10 June; another kite remained through the summer in San Diego County, where nesting eventually may occur. AB 37(6):1023, 1027, 1983.

Colorado

The city park at Lamar hosted at least 25 kites on 4 July and 48 on 26 July. AB 34(6):915, 1980. Mississippi Kites wandered 50–100 miles north and west of the nesting grounds to Ft. Morgan, 21 August, and Rye, 1 October. AB 38(2):228, 1984. A Mississippi Kite cruised over the interstate highway in downtown Pueblo, 23 August. AB 39(1):83, 1985. Mississippi Kites arrived at Lamar, 8 May. AB 39(3): 331, 1985. The city park at Lamar boasted 55 kites on 17 May, probably the highest count ever achieved in one location in Colorado. AB 40(3):503, 1986. Kites have spread up the Arkansas River to Pueblo, where 10–12 pairs nested at two places in the city. AB 41(5):1468, 1987. A Mississippi Kite perched on a power line in residential Denver, 4 July, perhaps scouting for [nesting?] sites like those kites occupy in the southern cities of Pueblo, LaJunta, and Lamar. AB 43(5):1346, 1989. The highest count yet for Pueblo, 30 kites, recorded 18 August. AB 44(1): 131, 1990.

Delaware

On 6 June, a Mississippi Kite soaring over the Lewes ferry terminal became the state's first record. AB 36(5):834, 1982. Unusual sighting of a kite near Dover, 26 May, the third record for the state. AB 38(5): 890, 1984.

Florida

A kite at St. Petersburg, 20 September, was unusual, as even in migration the species is rare in the peninsula south of Gainesville, its southern breeding limit. AB 36(2):169, 1982. Two adults south of Ocala, 22 and 28 May, suggest a possible southern range extension. AB 37(5): 861, 1983. Kites again in Ocala during the nesting season; a pair observed copulating near Madison, 5 May. AB 38(5):901, 1984. On 24 September, 20 Mississippi Kites recorded flying near Tallahassee, and two rare sightings south of Gainesville in early October. AB 39(1):43, 1985. A Mississippi Kite, rarely seen in southern Florida, was flying over Everglades National Park, 17 May. AB 42(3):424, 1988. On 2 August, 50 kites over Paynes Prairie made a very high count for the peninsula. AB 43(1):91, 1989. A kite nest near Cedar Key marked a southern extension of breeding. AB 43(5):1308, 1989. A kite hunted daily at the South Florida Research Center, 16–19 October; was it a trans-Gulf migrant, or wintering? AB 44(1):79, 1990. A kite arrived at Key West, 9 May. [From which direction? If from the south, this record suggests a trans-Gulf migrant.] A flock of 13 in Wakulla County, 6 May, indicated an increase in breeding in that area. AB 44(3):415, 1990. A Mississippi Kite nest at Ocala, 11 June, confirmed suspicions of several years. AB 45(1):92, 1991.

Georgia

Quite late for Georgia was a Mississippi Kite at Augusta, 1 October. AB 38(2):189, 1984.

Illinois

An extralimital Mississippi Kite appeared in Chicago, 14–15 June. AB 37(6):993, 1983. Record for Chicago, 18 May. AB 41(3):438, 1987.

Indiana

A Mississippi Kite at Willow Slough, 19 August, was exceptional. AB 34(2):167, 1980. An unexpected adult appeared at Little Cedar Lake. AB 38(5):1025, 1984. Two kites were discovered as Salamonie River State Forest, 10 June; single birds sighted at Richmond, 31 May to 4 June. AB 41(5):1441, 1987.

Iowa

A Mississipi Kite at Dudgeon Lake, 5–7 June, was joined by a second on 8–9 June. AB 43(5):1322, 1989. A kite sighted at Coralville Reservoir, 19 May, one of the few recent records for the state. AB 44(3):434, 1990. Two Mississippi Kites in Clive County, 22 June to 31 July, built a nest, but produced no eggs. The closest established breeding population is more than 300 miles from this location. AB 45(5):1121, 1991.

Louisiana

A Mississippi Kite at Baton Rouge on 10 December would be by 8 days the latest record for the state, and the more remarkable as this species is usually gone by mid-September. AB 39(2):176, 1985. A kite on 27 February was undoubtedly an early migrant. AB 34(3):280, 1980. Some 1,422 Mississippi Kites recorded at Baton Rouge during the fall, with 1,342 of these seen 19 August to 3 September. AB 44(1):105, 1990.

Maine

An immature Mississippi Kite at Lubec, 25 May, furnished an overdue first state record. AB 45(3):416, 1991.

Maryland

Two adults at Talbot County, 9 July, the second state record. AB 36(6):963, 1982. Reports of kites included immatures at Patuxent Wildlife Research Center, 3 June, and at Lanham, 27 June. AB 41(5):1419, 1987. Unprecedented sightings of three Mississippi Kites; singles at Ft. Smallwood State Park, 28 April, Huntley Meadows County Park, 8 May, and Rockville on 11 May. AB 44(3);408, 1990.

Massachusetts

A kite was identified in Chatham, 25 June. AB 34(6):875, 1980. Adult seen at Chatham, 6 May, and likely the same bird a day later at Truro. AB 37(5):846, 1983. A Mississippi Kite sighted at Bolton Flats, 14 September. AB 42(2):233, 1988. An "overshoot," at Granville, 27 April. AB 41(3):402, 1987. A subadult recorded at Provincetown and one dead at Martha's Vineyand, both 28 May. AB 42(3):408, 1988. Kites at Plymouth, 3 May, and Truro, 12 May. AB 44(3):397, 1990. Sightings at Cape Cod, *the* spot in New England for kite watching. AB 45(3):416, 1991. A sighting at Hingham, 8 June. AB 45(5):1093, 1991.

Michigan

Second state record at Kalamazoo in May. AB 38(5):913, 1984. Two Mississippi Kites, the fourth and fifth state records, on 23–24 May at Midland and 31 May at Whitefish Point Bird Observatory. AB 42(3): 437, 1988.

Minnesota

A third record of a Mississippi Kite came 25 May at Brown's Valley. AB 34(5):779, 1980. A fourth state record occurred at Oxbow Park in Olmstead County, 18 May. AB 35(5): 826, 1981.

Mississippi

Six kites seen flying over the business district in Petal, 9 August. AB 34(6):903, 1988.

Missouri

Extralimital kites appeared at Ted Shanks Wildlife Management Area during June. AB 38(6):1025, 1984. Two kites wandered into St. Joseph, 21 September. AB 41(1):95, 1987. Records for Jefferson City, 16 May, and West Plains, 24 May. AB 41(3):438, 1987. Mississippi Kites are expanding in Missouri; as many as six appeared near St. Louis, where a nest was located; 21 kites were counted within their traditional range along the Mississippi River in Union County, 6 July. AB 42(5):1294, 1988. An unprecedented movement of 300 kites on 16 May, including 150 in New Madrid County. These numbers exceed previous maxima for the region by a factor of ten. AB 45(3):452, 1991.

Nebraska

A major influx of Mississippi Kites occurred, with sightings in Hamilton, Polk, and Sarpy counties in early September. AB 38(2):219, 1984. Sightings included three kites in northeast Nebraska, 26–28 September. AB 41(1):110, 1987. Two Mississippi Kites sighted in Hamilton County. AB 43(1):125, 1989. An immature kite was injured by hail in Lancaster County; it was rehabilitated and later released. AB 45(1): 123, 1991.

Nevada

A Mississippi Kite at Alamo on 21 March performed graceful cork-screw aerobatics for 5 minutes, for the second state record. AB 36(5): 878, 1982.

New Jersey

Some six to seven sightings late May to early June, followed by an adult seen at Wildwood Crest on 1 August; speculation continues about nesting in Cumberland and Salem counties. AB 34(6):879, 1980. Four kites at Cape May for the fifth year in a row, including the latest ever, 25 September. AB 38(2):182, 1984. Two kites around Cape May until 6 June, as usual now since 1979. AB 39(5):891, 1985. A Mississippi Kite was unexpectedly seen at the New Jersey end of the Tacony-Palmyra Bridge to Philadelphia, 2 June. AB 42(5):1274, 1988. After a puny invasion, up to five kites were still present at Cape May, early June; the last was seen 14 June, without evidence of nesting. AB 41(5): 1415, 1987. An early Mississipi Kite sighted along the Garden State Parkway at Toms River on 27 April. AB 43(3):456, 1989. A kite seen repeatedly at Budd Lake in Morris County, late June through July. AB 43(5):1295, 1989. Usual late-spring flight at Cape May was comple-mented by sightings at Sandy Hook, 1 and 9 May, and two to four in Bergen County, 24 May. AB 44(3):402, 1990. In addition to the usual influx at Cape May, a kite was seen in Middlesex County on 13 May. AB 45(1):423, 1991.

New York

Two kites at Forest Park, Queens County, 3 May, represented the sec-ond record for the state. AB 37(5):852, 1983. A Mississippi Kite sighted at Braddock Bay on the shore of Lake Ontario, 22 April; another, possibly the same bird, recorded in Cattaraugus County, 20 April. AB 39(3):297, 1985. A single kite recorded at Forest Park, Queens, 24 May. AB 42(3):414, 1988. A Mississippi Kite was far afield at Great Gull Island off the eastern tip of Long Island, 25 May. AB 45(3):422, 1991.

North Carolina

A Mississippi Kite was seen at Buxton on the Outer Banks, 6 October. AB 36(2):166, 1982. An adult at Avon on 29 May and later on the same day at Bodie Island provided the first spring record for the Outer

Banks. AB 36(5):841, 1982. A record of 36 kites, all apparently adults, counted in a single flock at their usual breeding (?) spot near Scotland Neck, 3 June. AB 37(6):978, 1983. [A population of this size remains typical for this area, although, as of 1992, a nest has yet to be located.] Possibly the earliest arrival for the state included seven kites in Halifax County, 28 April, and a rear migrant near Swansboro on 16 May. AB 38(5):897, 1984. Two "overshooting" kites turned up at Raven Rock on 13 May and at Buxton on 14 May. AB 42(3):421, 1988. Kites reported in "new" areas, but no nests discovered. AB 45(5):1108, 1991.

Ohio

An immature Mississippi Kite along Lake Erie in Luca County on 11 May provided the second documented record for Ohio. AB 39(3):306, 1985. Single birds sighted at Fort Loramie, 3 June, and Delaware County, 23–24 June. AB 41(5):1441, 1987.

Oklahoma

At Oklahoma City, young kites and their nests have been removed so people may enter and leave their homes in safety. AB 38(6):1035, 1984. Mississippi Kites at Ponca City frequently chased Chimney Swifts, but never were observed catching any. AB 40(5):1222, 1986.

Pennsylvania

A noteworthy record at Morgan Hill, 23 April, and a first record for the western region, 15 May. AB 42(3):414, 434, 1988.

Rhode Island

An "overshoot," at Crunston [Cranston], on 27 May, the second state record. AB 41(3):402, 1987. A kite sighted at Briggs Beach, 26 August, provided the fifth state record (and the third this year). AB 44(1):56, 1990.

South Carolina

Likely the first nesting record for Sumpter occurred when a pair of kites nested above a home in a residential area. AB 40(5):1192, 1986. [This is a rare instance of kites nesting in urban locations in the eastern United States, although we anticipate more of these occurrences in the years ahead.] A kite in Fairfield County represents a rare sighting in the Piedmont. AB 43(2):300, 1989.

Texas

At least two pairs nested in El Paso. AB 34(6):909, 1980. Between 23 and 28 May, 30 Mississippi Kites flew daily around a bank building in Amarillo, presumably feeding on the plentiful "miller moths." AB 36(5):869, 1982. Five pairs of kites nesting at a golf course at El Paso were so belligerent that their nests were destroyed (legally). AB 37(6): 1002, 1983. A very late kite was well described in Houston on 12 December. AB 38(3):334, 1984. A golfer at Midland required four stitches to mend a scalp wound administered by a Mississippi Kite. AB 38(6): 1035, 1984. Three kites in Houston, 25 February, were 3 weeks earlier than normal for northbound migrants. AB 39(2):186, 1985. Mississippi Kites continue to harass golfers and homeowners passing near nests; at Fort Worth, kites were observed catching Purple Martins. AB 39(5):932, 1985. Some 41 kites were in two trees in Fort Worth, 25 August. AB 40(1):135, 1986. An extremely early kite flew over Dallas County, 27 February. AB 40(2):308, 1986. A spectacular flight of 600 kites over Uvalde, 4 May, the largest flock of the season. AB 40(3):495, 1986. A Mississippi Kite in Grimes, 26 February, was very early. AB 41(2):298, 1987. Kites continue to be seen with increasing frequency throughout much of the Panhandle and northcentral regions; 100 were seen in Hall County, 2 July. AB 42(5):1312, 1988. As many as 40 kites reported nesting in residential areas in San Angelo. AB 43(3):505, 1989. A Mississippi Kite arriving in Lubbock on 3 March was extremely early; this is the third year in a row with a sighting in March. AB 45(3):470, 1991.

Virginia

The first confirmed record occurred near Leesburg, 6–7 June; a tame kite chased a Chimney Swift and fed on 17-year cicadas. AB 41(5): 1419, 1987. A kite observed at False Cape State Park at Virginia Beach, 20 May. AB 42(3):417, 1988. A Mississippi Kite at Highland on 23 June still was the best raptor record for the season. AB 42(5):1287, 1988. Two adults, 21 June, represent one of the few records for the Delmarava Peninsula. AB 45(5):1102, 1991.

Wisconsin

Ninth record of a Mississippi Kite in the state occurred near Lake Michigan on 5 June. AB 34(6):897, 1980. A rare sighting of a kite at leisure, hawking for insects along the Mississippi River at Eagle Valley Nature Centure, 6 September. AB 36(2):180, 1982. A dead kite was found in the fall at Kaukauna's Thousand Islands Wildlife Area. AB 37(2):183, 1983. A kite was seen 25 June in Dane County. AB 39(5):915, 1985. A sighting at Sheboygan, 7 June. AB 41(5):1438, 1987. A Mississippi Kite observed migrating along the Lake Michigan shore at Concorida College, 20 September. AB 43(1):105, 1989.

Ontario, Canada

An adult Mississippi Kite at Pelee, 17–21 May, is the province's thirteenth record, nine of which have occurred since 1980. AB 45(3): 441, 1991.

Readings and References

*L*iterature concerning the Mississippi Kite is not extensive when compared with that for such species as Kestrels, Mallards, or Meadowlarks, but even so, space prohibits a full listing of the scattered literature about Mississippi Kites. Nevertheless, those works cited here suffice as an entry point for readers who wish to learn more about this beautiful "southern hawk" and other raptors. We especially commend the works of James W. Parker, whose field experience with Mississippi Kites is unmatched.

General

Bent, A. C. 1937. Life histories of North American birds of prey. Part 1, U.S. Nat. Mus. Bull. 167, Smithsonian Inst., Washington, D.C. [Reprinted in 1961 by Dover, NY.]

Brown, L. 1976. Birds of prey, their biology and ecology. Hamlyn Publ. Co., N.Y.

Brown, L., and D. Amadon. 1968. Eagles, hawks and falcons of the world. Vol. 1. McGraw-Hill Book Co., N.Y.

Craighead, J. J., and F. C. Craighead, Jr. 1956. Hawks, owls and wildlife. Wildl. Manage. Inst., Washington, D.C.

Glinski, R. L., and A. L. Gennaro. 1988. Mississippi Kite. Pages 54–56 *in* R. L. Glinski et al., eds. Proc. SW Raptor Manage. Sympos. and Workshop, Nat. Wildl. Federation Sci. Tech. Series No. 11.

Meyer, K. D. 1990. Kites. Pages 38–49 *in* B. G. Pendleton, ed. Proc. SE Raptor Manage. Sympos. and Workshop, Nat. Wildl. Federation Sci. Tech. Series No. 14.

Oberholser, H. C. 1974. The bird life of Texas. E. B. Kincaid, Jr., ed. Univ. Texas Press, Austin.

Palmer, R. S. 1988. Handbook of North American birds. Vol. 4. Yale Univ. Press, New Haven. [Included are several sections by James W. Parker.]

Sutton, G. M. 1967. Oklahoma birds. Univ. Oklahoma Press, Norman.

Breeding and Nesting Ecology

Bendire, C. 1892. Life histories of North American birds, with special reference to their breeding habits and eggs. Vol. 1, U.S. Nat. Mus. Special Bull. 1, Smithsonian Inst., Washington, D.C.

Cely, J. E. 1987. American Swallow-tailed Kite used Mississippi Kite nest. J. Raptor Res. 21:124.

Evans, S. A. 1981. Ecology and behavior of the Mississippi Kite (*Ictinia mississippiensis*) in southern Illinois. M.S. thesis, Southern Illinois Univ., Carbondale. 116pp.

Fitch, H. S. 1963. Observations on the Mississippi Kite in southwestern Kansas. Mus. Nat. Hist. 12:503–519, Univ. Kansas Publ., Lawrence.

Ganier, A. F. 1902. The Mississippi Kite (*Ictinia mississippiensis*). Osprey 1:85–90.

Glinski, R., and R. D. Ohmart. 1983. Breeding ecology of the Mississippi Kite in Arizona. Condor 85:200–207.

Jackson, A. S. 1945. Mississippi Kites. Texas Game and Fish 3:6–7.

Love, D., J. A. Grzybowski, and F. L. Knopf. 1985. Influence of various land uses on windbreak selection by nesting Mississippi Kites. Wilson Bull. 97:561–565.

Parker, J. W. 1974. The breeding biology of the Mississippi Kite in the Great Plains. Ph.D. dissertation. Univ. Kansas, Lawrence. 207pp.

Parker, J. W. 1981. Nest associates of the Mississippi Kite. J. Field Ornithol. 52:144–145.

Robinson, T. S. 1957. Notes on the development of a brood of Mississippi Kites in Barber County, Kansas. Trans. Kansas Acad. Sci. 60:174–180.

Sutton, G. M. 1939. The Mississippi Kite in spring. Condor 41:41–53.

Wolfe, L. R. 1967. The Mississippi Kite in Texas. Bull. Texas Ornithol. Soc. 1:2–3, 12–13.

See also citations elsewhere for Gennaro (1988a) and Shaw (1985).

Distribution and Status

Kalla, P. I. and F. J. Alsop III. 1983. The distribution, habitat preference, and status of the Mississippi Kite in Tennessee. Am. Birds 37:146–149.

Merriam, C. H. 1898. Life zones and crop zones of the United States. Bull. 10, Bureau Biol. Survey, U.S. Dep. Agric., Washington, D.C.

Parker, J. W. 1975. Populations of the Mississippi Kite in the Great Plains. Pages 159–173 *in* J. R. Murphy, C. M. White, and B. E. Harrell, eds. Proc. Conf. Raptor Conserv. Techniques, Raptor Res. Rep. No. 3, Raptor Res. Foundation, Vermillion, S.D.

Parker, J. W., and J. C. Ogden. 1979. The recent history and status of the Mississippi Kite. Am. Birds 33:119–129. [A major review of distribution up to date of issue.]

Food Habits

Glinski, R. L., T. G. Grubb, and L. A. Forbis. 1983. Snag use by selected raptors. Pages 130–133 *in* Snag habitat management: proceedings of the symposium. U.S. Dep. Agric. Forest Service General Tech. Rep. RM-99. Rocky Mt. Forest and Range Exp. Sta., Fort Collins, Colo.

Glinski, R. L., and R. D. Ohmart. 1984. Factors of reproduction and population densities of the Apache cicada (*Diceroprocta apache*). Southwestern Nat. 29:73–79.

Hobbs, J. N. 1986. Black Kites and other raptors feeding on cicadas. Aust. Birds 20:87–88.

Parker, J. W. 1982. Opportunistic feeding by an ornate box turtle under the nest of a Mississippi Kite. Southwestern Nat. 27:365.

Skinner, R. W. 1962. Feeding habits of the Mississippi Kite. Auk 79:273–274.

Snyder, N. F. R., and J. W. Wiley. 1976. Sexual size dimorphism in hawks and owls of North America. Ornithol. Monogr. 20, Am. Ornithol. Union. [A full examination of the puzzle about why female raptors are usually larger than males, with an emphasis on feeding ecology.]

Storer, R. W. 1966. Sexual dimorphism and food habits in three North American accipiters. Auk 83:423–436.

Wayne, A. T. 1906. A contribution to the ornithology of South Carolina, chiefly the coast region. Auk 23:56–68.

See also citations elsewhere for Fitch (1963), Glinski and Ohmart (1983), Jackson (1945), Robinson (1957), and Sutton (1939).

Geographical Records

Carothers, S. W., and R. R. Johnson. 1976. The Mississippi Kite in Arizona: a second record. Condor 78:114–115.

Connor, J. 1991. Season at the point: the birds and birders of Cape May. Atlantic Monthly Press, New York.

Cranson, B. F. 1975. Population status of the Mississippi Kite in Colorado. Pages 173–176 *in* J. R. Murphy, C. M. White, and B. E. Harrell, eds. Proc. Conf. Raptor Conserv. Techniques, Raptor Res. Rep. No. 3, Raptor Res. Foundation, Vermillion, S.D.

LeGrand, H. E., Jr., and J. M. Lynch. 1973. Mississippi Kites in northeastern North Carolina. Chat 37:105–106.

Levy, S. H. 1971. The Mississippi Kite in Arizona. Condor 73:476.

Rea, A. M. 1983. Once a river: bird life and habitat changes on the Middle Gila. Univ. Arizona Press, Tucson.

See also Breeding and Nesting.

Helpers at the Nest

Mader, W. J. 1979. Breeding behavior of a polyandrous trio of Harris' Hawks in southern Arizona. Auk 96:776–788.

Parker, J. W. and M. Ports. 1982. Helping at the nest by yearling Mississippi Kites. Raptor Res. 16:14–17.

Woolfenden, G. E. 1975. Florida scrub jay helpers at the nest. Auk 92:1–15.

Woolfenden, G. E. 1976. Co-operative breeding in American birds. Proc. 16th Int. Ornithol. Congr.:674–684.

History and Conservation

Audubon, J. J. 1840. The birds of America. Vol. 1. Chevalier, Philadelphia.

Baird, S. F. 1858. Birds, reports of explorations and surveys. Vol. IX, House Ex. Doc. 91, 33rd Congr., 2nd sess. [This work summarizes the ornithology of the Pacific railroad surveys of the 1850s.]

Bolen, E. G. and D. L. Flores. 1989. The Mississippi Kite in the environmental history of the southern Great Plains. Prairie Nat. 21:65–74.

Brett, J. J. 1991. The mountain and the migration: a guide to Hawk Mountain. Rev. ed. Cornell Univ. Press, Ithaca, N.Y. 114pp.

Brett, J. J. and A. C. Nagy. 1973. Feathers in the wind: the mountain and the migration. Hawk Mountain Sanctuary Assoc., Kempton, Penn.

Cade, T. J. 1983. Snake River Birds of Prey Area. Pages 113–115 *in* S. A. Temple, ed. Bird conservation 1. International Council for Bird Preservation, United States Section, Univ. Wisconsin Press, Madison.

Carroll, H. B., ed. 1941. The journal of Lieutenant J. W. Abert from Bent's Fort to St. Louis in 1845. Panhandle-Plains Historical Society, Canyon, Tex.

Cramp, S. 1977. The problems facing birds of prey—the view of ornithologists and conservationists. World Conf. Birds of Prey 1:9–11.

Flores, D. L. 1984a. The ecology of the Red River in 1806: Peter Custis and early southwestern natural history. Southwestern Hist. Quart. 88:1–42.

Flores, D. L., ed. 1984b. Jefferson & southwestern exploration: the Freeman & Custis accounts of the Red River Expedition of 1806. Univ. Oklahoma Press, Norman. [A full history of a noteworthy but overlooked expedition, including reproduction of the journal that contains the first known description of the Mississippi Kite.]

Ford, A. ed. 1969. Audubon, by himself. Natural History Press, Garden City, N.Y.

Foreman, G., ed. 1941. A pathfinder in the southwest; the itinerary of Lieutenant A. W. Whipple. Univ. Oklahoma Press, Norman.

Fuller, H., and L. Hafen, eds. 1957. The journal of Captain John R. Bell. *In* R. G. Thwaites, ed. Early western travels. Arthur H. Clark Co., Glendale, Calif.

Graham, F., Jr. 1990. The Audubon ark: a history of the National Audubon Society. Alfred A. Knopf, New York.

Harris, D. 1971. Recent plant invasions in the arid and semi-arid Southwest of the United States. Pages 459–481 *in* T. Detwyler, ed. Man's impact on the environment. McGraw-Hill, New York.

Herriek, F. H. 1938. Audubon the naturalist: a history of his life and time. 2nd ed. Appleton-Century, New York.

Hornaday, W. T. 1913. Our vanishing wild life: its extermination and preservation. New York Zool. Soc., New York. [Reprinted in 1970 by Arno Press & The New York Times, New York.]

Jackson, D., ed. 1966. The journals of Zebulon Montgomery Pike. 2 vols. Univ. Oklahoma Press, Norman.

Kochert, M. N., and M. Pellant. 1986. Multiple use in the Snake River Birds of Prey Area. Rangelands 8:217–220.

McCauley, A. H. 1988. Notes on the ornithology of the region about the source of the Red River of Texas. K. Seyffert and T. L. Baker, eds. Panhandle-Plains Hist. Rev. 61:25–88.

Mollhausen, B. 1858. Diary of a journey from the Mississippi to the coasts of the Pacific with a United States government expedition. 2 vols. Longmans, Brown, Green, Longmans and Roberts, London.

Nuttall, T. 1979. A journal of travels into the Arkansas Territory in the year 1819. S. Lottinville, ed. Univ. Oklahoma Press, Norman.

Senner, S. E. 1989. Hawk Mountain Sanctuary Association, Pennsylvania. Am. Birds 43:248–253.

Simpson, M. B., Jr., and D. S. McAllister. 1986. Alexander Wilson's southern tour of 1809: the North Carolina transit and subscribers to the *American Ornithology.* N.C. Hist. Rev. 63:421–476.

Stone, W. 1965. Bird studies at old Cape May. Vol. 1. Dover, New York. [The original work was published in 1937 by the Delaware Valley Ornithological Club, but the Dover reprint includes a valuable introduction by the dean of American birders, R. T. Peterson, and a biographical sketch of Dr. Stone.]

Weese, A. C., ed. 1947. The journal of Titian Ramsey Peale, pioneer naturalist. Missouri Hist. Rev. 41:147–163, 266–284.

Wilson, A. 1811. American ornithology. Vol. 3. [See Brewer, T. M., 1840. Wilson's American ornithology. Otis, Broaders, and Co., Boston. Reprinted in 1970 by Arno Press & The New York Times, New York.]

Woodhouse, Samuel Washington. Papers. Manuscript Collection 387B. Acad. Nat. Sci. of Philadelphia. Philadelphia.

Migration

Davis, S. E. 1989. Migration of the Mississippi Kite *Ictinia mississippiensis* in Bolivia, with comments on *I. plumbea.* Bull. British Ornithol. Club 109:149–152.

Eubanks, T. R. 1971. Unusual flight of Mississippi Kites in Payne County, Oklahoma. Bull. Okla. Ornithol. Soc. 4:33.

Heintzelman, D. S. 1986. The migrations of hawks. Indiana Univ. Press, Bloomington.

Kerlinger, P. 1989. Flight strategies of migrating hawks. Univ. Chicago Press, Chicago.

Kerlinger, P., and S. A. Gauthreaux, Jr. 1985. Flight behavior of raptors during spring migration in south Texas studied with radar and visual observations. J. Field Ornithol. 56:394–402.

Lathbury, G. 1968. Autumn migration of raptors across the Straits of Gibraltar. Ibis 110:210–211.

Lowery, G. H., Jr. 1946. Evidence for trans-Gulf migration. Auk 63:175–211.

Orr, R. T. 1970. Animals in migration. Macmillan, New York.

Thiollay, J. M. 1977. La migration d'automne sur la cote orientale du Mexique. Alauda 45:344–346.

Thiollay, J. M. 1979. L'importance d'un axe de migration: la coste est due Mexique. Alauda 47:236–245.

Nestlings and Juveniles

Ingram, C. 1959. The importance of juvenile cannibalism in the breeding biology of certain birds of prey. Auk 76:218–226.

Robinson, T. S. 1957. Notes on the development of a brood of Mississippi Kites in Barber County, Kansas. Trans. Kansas Acad. Sci. 60:174–180.

See also Fitch (1963) regarding food habits of young kites.

Pesticides

Hickey, J. J., and D. W. Anderson. 1968. Chlorinated hydrocarbons and eggshell changes in raptorial and fish-eating birds. Science 162:271–273. [One of the influential papers about the relationship between pesticides and the decline of certain species of birds.]

Parker, J. W. 1976. Pesticides and eggshell thinning in the Mississippi Kite. J. Wildl. Manage. 40:243–248.

Predation

Errington, P. L. 1967. Of predation and life. Iowa State Univ. Press, Ames.

Flader, S. L. 1974. Thinking like a mountain: Aldo Leopold and the evolution of an ecological attitude toward deer, wolves, and forests. Bison Books, Univ. Nebraska Press, Lincoln. [See also Thinking like a mountain, in Leopold's enduring collection of essays entitled A sand county almanac and sketches here and there, first published in 1949 and now widely reprinted.]

Mech, D. L. 1966. The wolves of Isle Royale. U.S. Nat. Park Serv. Faunal Series No. 7.

Rudebeck, G. 1951. The choice of prey and modes of hunting of predatory birds with special reference to their selective effect. Oikos 3: 200–231.

Taxonomy, Nomenclature, and Common Names

American Ornithologists' Union. 1983. Check-list of North American birds. 6th ed. American Ornithologists' Union, Washington, D.C. [This is the authoritive source for the nomenclature of North American birds; revised editions have been published intermittently since 1886.]

Brown, L., and D. Amadon. 1968. Eagles, hawks, and falcons of the world. Vol. 1. McGraw-Hill, New York.

Cassin, J. 1856. Illustrations of the birds of California, Texas, Oregon, British and Russian America. J. B. Lippincott, Philadelphia. 298pp. [Reprinted in 1991 by the Texas State Historical Assoc., Austin.]

Kalmbach, E. R. 1968. American bird names/their histories and meanings. Auk 85:703–706. [A special review of W. L. McAtee's 1,697-page manuscript housed in the Olin Library at Cornell University, Ithaca, N.Y.]

Urban Ecology

Bolen, E. G. 1991. Analogs: a concept for the research and management of urban wildlife. Landscape and Urban Plann. 20:285–289.

Engle, M. C. 1980. Mississippi Kite strikes human being. Bull. Oklahoma Ornithol. Soc. 13:21–22.

Gennaro, A. L. 1988a. Breeding biology of an urban population of Mississippi Kites in New Mexico. Pages 188–190 *in* R. L. Glinski et al., eds. Proc. SW Raptor Manage. Sympos. and Workshop, Nat. Wildl. Federation Sci. Tech. Series No. 11.

Gennaro, A. L. 1988b. Extent and control of aggressive behavior toward humans by Mississippi Kites. Pages 249–252 *in* R. L. Glinski et al., eds. Proc. SW Raptor Manage. Sympos. and Workshop, Nat. Wildl. Federation Sci. Tech. Series No. 11.

Parker, J. W. 1987. Urban-nesting Mississippi Kites: history, problems, management, and benefits. Pages 232–234 *in* L. W. Adams and D. L. Leedy, eds. Integrating man and nature in the metropolitan environment, Nat. Inst. Urban Wildl., Columbia, Md.

Parker, J. W. 1988. The ace dive-bomber of the prairie is terror on the green. Smithsonian 19(4):54–60, 62–63.

Shaw, D. 1985. The breeding biology of urban-nesting Mississippi Kites (*Ictinia mississippiensis*) in west central Texas. M.S. thesis. Angelo State Univ., San Angelo, Tex. 52pp.

Territoriality

Nice, M. M. 1941. The role of territory in bird life. Am. Midland Nat. 26:441–487. [A pioneering study worthy of review, but readers should refer to more current works for a fuller knowledge of this complex topic in birds.]

Wintering Areas

Davis, S. E. 1989. Migration of the Mississippi Kite *Ictina mississippiensis* in Bolivia, with Comments on *I. plumbea*. Bull. Brit. Ornithol. Club 109:149–152.

Eisenmann, E. 1963. Mississippi Kite in Argentina; with comments on migration and plumages in the genus *Ictinia*. Auk 80:74–77.

Parker, J. W. 1977. Second record of the Mississipi Kite in Guatemala. Auk 94:168–169.

Shaw, D., and T. C. Maxwell. 1988. First record of the Mississippi Kite for Bolivia. J. Raptor Res. 22:90.